Copyright © 2023 by Little Publishing, LLC.

All rights reserved. No portion of this book may be reproduced-mechanically, electronically, or by any other means, including photocopying-without written permission of the publisher.

Dr. Ashley Little
Editor-In-Chief

LETTERS FROM OUR EDITORS

CREATING YOUR SEAT AT THE *Table*

A LETTER FROM OUR EDITOR-IN-CHIEF

Welcome!! to Creating Your Seat At The Table International Magazine. I am super excited to bring another amazing platform to you. This magazine will provide content geared toward spreading awareness and helping change the narrative. This issue will feature powerful leaders throughout the world who are breaking glass ceilings and blazing trails nationally and internationally. We will feature sections such as HERstory, Hidden Figure, Women On The Move, and much more. This online and in-print magazine was created with the Entrepreneur/Authorpreneur/Mompreneur/Celebrity/Influencer in mind.

It is important for us to build our own tables and create room for others at the table. It is important for us to use our voices and share our stories to help someone else along the way. A successful leader reaches back and help others which is the definition of true success. This magazine will feature experts throughout the world nationally and internationally who are doing great things and are making great change in their respective industries. **CREATE YOUR SEAT AT THE TABLE!!**

We can ALL WIN!!!

Dr. Ashley Little
CEO/Editor-In-Chief
Creating Your Seat at The Table Magazine

A LETTER FROM OUR ASSISTANT EDITOR-IN-CHIEF

Dearly Beloved Reading Audience,

I'm so excited to be a part of the Creating Your Seat at The Table editorial family. Ashley has put together what I would dare to define as a "masterpiece" of a magazine. From the writers, to the featured articles, even down to the sponsors, EVERYTHING was meticulously orchestrated to bring you the BEST for your eyes to behold! The goal is to always provide you with life changing content that will cause you to level up and take ACTION in each area of your life! No more living mediocre!

Please be on the look out for how you can partner with the Creating Your Seat at The Table movement and become a published author, start a profitable business, get amazing inspiring products, or get coached by Master Coach Dr. Ashley Little herself.

We are living in the best of times and worse of times. However, I do believe we are in a time that our ancestors would be proud of us. It's true, "If we fight, we WILL win!"

Be encouraged! Stay FOCUSED! The best is YET to come!

See You at The Top,

Dr. Jessica L. Mosley
Assistant Editor-In-Chief
Creating Your Seat at The Table Magazine

Dr. Jessica L. Mosley
Assistant Editor-In-Chief

ASHLEYLITTLEENTERPRISES.COM

Meet
DR. ASHLEY LITTLE
CHIEF EDITOR

Dr. Ashley Little is Ms. Georgia Global Continental 2023 and the CEO/Founder of Ashley Little Enterprises, LLC, which encompasses her media, consulting work, writing, ghost writing, book publishing, book coaching, project management, magazine, public relations & marketing, and empowerment speaking. In addition, she is an award-winning serial entrepreneur, TV/radio host, TEDx speaker, international speaker, keynote speaker, media maven, journalist, writer, host, philanthropist, business coach, investor, advisor for She Wins Society, and 21-times award-winning bestselling author. As seen on Black Enterprise (2X), *Forbes* (2X), *Sheen Magazine* (Print and Online), Sheen Talk, Voyage ATL, Fox Soul TV, NBC, Fox, CBS, BlackNews.Com, Shoutout Miami, Shoutout Atlanta, Morning Star, Yahoo Finance, Heart and Soul, The Book of Sean, *HBCU Times*, *VIP Global Magazine*, The Black Report, Vocal, Ted.com, Medium, Soul Wealth, Hustle and Soul, BlackBusiness.com, Glambitious Top 21 Women Of 2021, New York Weekly's Top 10 Hardest Working CEOs alongside billionaire Mark Cuban, *US Insider's* Top 10 Women Entrepreneurs alongside billionaire and media mogul, Oprah Winfrey, *London Daily Post*, *Sheen Magazine* 5 Pioneers Making a Difference in Their Communities, NCA&T *Alumni Times*, CEO Weekly Top 10 Influential People in 2021 alongside billionaires Jeff Bezos and Beyonce' and many more. Through the Biden & Harris Administration, and Leaders Esteem Christian Bible University, she was also awarded with the Presidential Lifetime Achievement Award the highest award in the country. She is a board member for Leaders Esteem Christian Bible University, as well. Charter member for Dr. Judy Rashid Leadership and Education Center in South Africa.

As a recipient of the "Author of The Year" award by Glambitious, she is also a part of The Forbes Next 1000 Class of 2021 in partnership with Square. This first-of-its-kind initiative celebrates bold and inspiring entrepreneurs who are redefining what it means to run a business. Furthermore, she was a recipient of Nashville's Black 40 Under 40 Awards in December 2021. It is an annual event honoring the best and the brightest for their accomplishments in their chosen field and for their contributions and commitment to the African American

ASHLEYLITTLEENTERPRISES.COM

MEET DR. ASHLEY LITTLE

community. Dr. Little is also an official member of For(bes) The Culture. For(bes) The Culture was formed in Boston at the Forbes Under 30 Summit in October of 2017. They pride themselves on convening current and future black and brown leaders worldwide to network, collaborate, share opportunities, and discuss issues related to their communities and the planet at-large. She was recognized along with other influential leaders and distinguished entrepreneurs, including Oprah Winfrey, Mel Robbins, Gary V and many more for the annual Brainz 500 Global Awards List awarded by *Brainz Magazine*. Lastly, she is a proud member of The Chancellor's Round Table at North Carolina A&T State University and 2022 Recipient of the Dr. Velma Speight Young Alumna Award at North Carolina A&T State University.

She is a proud member of Delta Sigma Theta Sorority, Incorporated, and a member of Alpha Phi Omega. She is very involved in her community, organizations and non-profits. Currently, she is the co-founder of Sweetheart Scholars non-profit organization, along with three other powerful women. This scholarship is given out annually to African American females from her hometown of Wadesboro, North Carolina who are attending college to help with their expenses. Dr. Little believes it takes a village to raise a child and she also encourages others to never forget where you come from. Dr. Little is a strong believer in giving back to her community. She believes our young ladies need vision, direction and strong mentorship. She is the CEO/Founder/Visionary Author of The HBCU Experience Movement, LLC, the first Black-owned company to launch books written and published by prominent alumni throughout the world who attended Historically Black Colleges & Universities (HBCUs). As authors, they share a powerful collection of stories on how their unique college experience has molded them into the people they are today. The purpose of The HBCU Experience Movement is to change the narrative by sharing Black stories and investing financially back into our HBCUs to increase young alumni giving and enrollment. The award-winning bestselling authors won the Black Authors Matter TV Award in May of 2021, Inaugural Anthem Awards of 2022, as well as the International Book Awards by The American Book Fest. The books are also part of the WorldCat.org, the world's largest network of library content and services. Dr. Little is also the Editor and Chief of *Creating Your Seat at The Table International Magazine*, advisor for She Wins Society, and writing and publishing coach for the WILDE Winner's Circle.

She is the founder and owner of T.A.L.K. Radio & TV Network, LLC, which airs in over 167 countries, and streams live on Facebook, YouTube, Twitter and Periscope. This broadcasting and media production company is for new or existing radio shows, television shows, or other electronic media outlets to air content from a centralized source. All news, information or music shared on this platform are solely the responsibility of the station/radio owner. She is also the owner and creator of Creative Broadcasting Radio Station, the station of "unlimited possibilities." She is also one of the hosts of the new TV Show *Daytime Drama* nationally syndicated television show, which will be aired on Comcast Channel 19 and AT&T Channel 99 in 19 middle Tennessee counties. It will also air on The United Broadcasting Network, The Damascus Roads Broadcasting Network, and Roku.

Dr. Little is a 21X award-winning bestselling author of, *Dear Fear, Volume 2: 18 Powerful Lessons of Living Your Best Life Outside of Fear*; *The Gyrlfriend Code, Volume 1*; *I Survived*; *Girl, Get Up and Win*; *Glambitious Guide to Being an Entrepreneur*; *The Price of Greatness*; *The Making of a Successful Business Woman*; and *Hello, Queen*. She is a co-host for The Tamie Collins Markee Radio Show, award-winning entrepreneur who is also a reflection contributor for the book, NC Girls Living in a Maryland World, Sales/Marketing/Contributing Writer/Event Correspondent for *SwagHer Magazine*, contributing writer for MizCEO Magazine, contributing editor for *SheIs Magazine*, contributing writer/national sales executive for *Courageous Woman Magazine*, contributing writer for Upwords International Magazine (India), and contributing writer/global partner for Powerhouse Global International Magazine(London). Host of "Creating Your Seat At The Table", Host of "Authors On The Rise", Co-Host Glambitious Podcast, Partner/Visionary Author of The Gyrlfriend Code The Sorority Edition along with The Gyrlfriend Collective, LLC. Lastly, she has received awards, such as "Author of the Month"; The Executive Citation of Anne Arundel County, Maryland Award, which was awarded by the County Executive Steuart L. Pittman; and Top 28 Influential Business Pioneers for *K.I.S.H. Magazine* Spring 2019 Edition. She

ASHLEYLITTLEENTERPRISES.COM

MEET DR. ASHLEY LITTLE

has been featured in *All About Inspire Magazine*, *Formidable Magazine*, *BRAG Magazine*, the front cover of *MizCEO Magazine* in November of 2019, the front cover for *Upwords Magazine* in the October 2019 Edition, *Courageous Woman* Special Speakers Edition in November 2019 and *Influence Magazine*. She has been featured on a nationally syndicated television show, *HBCU 101*, on Aspire TV, Dynasty of Dreamers *K.I.S.H. Magazine* Spring 2019 Edition, the front cover of *Courageous Magazine* in December of 2019, the front cover of *Doz International Magazine* in January 2020, Top 28 Influential Business Pioneers for *K.I.S.H. Magazine*, *Power20 Magazine Glambitious* January 2020 and *Power20 Magazine Glambitious* February 2020. She was also featured in *Powerhouse Global International London Magazine* March 2020 edition, *National Boss Magazine* in the October 2020 edition, *Sheen Magazine* February 2020 edition as one of "The Top 20 Women to Be on The Lookout for in 2020", BlackNews.com, BlackBusiness.com, the front cover of *She Speaks Magazine* August 2020 edition, as well as the front cover of *National Boss Magazine* November 2020 edition.

In addition, she's been featured on BlackNewsScoop.com, awarded the National Women's Empowerment Ministry "Young, Gifted & Black Award" in February 2020, which honors and celebrates women in business below age 40 for their creativity and business development. Featured in *National Women Empowerment Magazine*, *Black Enterprise*, as well as on Fox, NBC, and CBS, she was interviewed on *The Black Report* on Fox Soul TV and the front cover for *National Boss Magazine*. She was also a speaker at The Black College Expo 2020, for Creative CEOs Summit in January of 2021, and international speaker for Living Your Dream Life Summit 2021. She was also the speaker for the Elite Business Women Powershift Conference 2021, The Bella, The Brand & Her Bag Wealth Summit 2021, The Unstoppable You Summit in January 2021, the Marketing Mastery Summit for Glambitious 2021, the Crown Yourself Conference in January 2021, as well as the Door Dash Virtual Black History Month Celebration. As the speaker for Day of Aggie Generations with North Carolina A&T State University, Dr. Little was the 2021 Woman of Black Excellence Honoree, guest speaker on the podcast, The Happy Hour Show, speaker for the Phoenix Jack & Jill HBCU Author Showcase, as well as a guest on The JMosley Show. As contributing author for *Prayers for The Entrepreneurial Woman* book, she has spoken at Creative Con, been recognized as one of Today's Black History Makers, as well as being a featured speaker at From Paper to Profits Conference. She has been afforded the opportunity to gain press access for "Don't Waste Your Petty" movie as well as Mahalia Jackson's movie. She's been a speaker for HerStory Women's Global Empowerment Summit, HerStory Women Who Lead Conference, Stepping N2 Sisterhood Sharing Winning Secrets Virtual Summit, I AM Glambitious Virtual Conference, Black Authors Matter TV show, Thought Leaders Global Virtual Summit, as well as A Conversation with Floyd Marshall, Jr. As a Black Authors Matter TV award winner, Grind Pretty Magazine, Revolt. She has spoken for Sheen Talk and served as the foreword author for the anthology *It Cost to Be the Boss*. Recognized by *VIP Global Magazine* as one of the Top 50 Most Influential Women, she has spoken at Black Writers Weekend, The GameChangers with Angela Ward show, and served as keynote speaker for Blacks in Nonprofits Conference. Having served as speaker for the Leap Conference, Pass the Mic Sis, the From Purpose to Profit Summit, and The Been Worthy Podcast, she has been the speaker and host for the MizCEO graduation, was featured in *Emoir Magazine* for Building a Global Media Empire, Front Cover GlamCEO Magazine December 2022 and was a Making Black History Today recipient for Glambitious, 2023 Woman To Watch for Glambitious, 20 Black Women Entrepreneurs To Watch for BlkWomenHustle, Guest/Speaker on Glambitious Inaugural Live Talk Show Series, Model for Black Beauty Expo 2023, Recipient of The Champion Of Change Award from Colour Me Social Foundation, Black Women Making History for BlkWomenHustle, Speaker/Honoree at The Stepping N2 Sisterhood Conference 2023.

Dr. Little received her undergraduate degree in English from North Carolina A&T State University. She received her master's degree in Leadership and Coaching and her Doctorate in Leadership, as well. Dr. Little is a mover and shaker, and she continuously pushes herself to be better than she was yesterday. She gives God all the credit for everything that has happened in her life. She has strong faith and determination to be great. She believes her only competition is herself. Her favorite scripture is Philippians 4:13: "I can do all things through Christ who strengthens me."

Contributing Writers

Gracia Collins Rich

Nykole Wyatt

Dr. Nancy Dozier

Dr. Cozette M. White

Dr. Leslie Hodge

Danielle Marshall

Everold Reid

Dr. Kerry Ann-Zamore

Brittany Ramsey

Bailey Reese Moore

Kirby Wilson

CELEBRATING WOMEN'S HISTORY MONTH
CREATING YOUR SEAT AT THE *table*

INSIDE THIS ISSUE

COVER STORY
CHRISTY RUTHERFORD

Women's Leadership Expert, Christy Rutherford's, aim is to lead women into the future of entrepreneurship and financial freedom. She provides them with the resources to navigate workplace politics while creating self-awareness and confidence to ASK for the compensation they truly deserve.

10.

COVER STORY
MONEI SUTTON

Movie Director, Model, Entrepreneur, Radio Host and Former Miss Teen USA. Monei Sutton, is a modern Renaissance Woman. Hailing from Atlanta, Georgia, Monei brings her God-given talents to all ventures she embarks on.

14.

30. Million Dollar Moguls

Jasmine Womack

32. Million Dollar Moguls

Dee Edward Fomby

ASHLEYLITTLEENTERPRISES.COM

INSIDE THIS ISSUE

CREATING YOUR SEAT AT THE TABLE

March 2023

Dr. Ashley Little
Editor-In-Chief

Dr. Jessica Mosley
Assistant Editor-In-Chief

Advertising
aalittle08@gmail.com

ashleylittleenterprises.com
info@ashleyalittle.com

Published quarterly by
Little Publishing LLC
All Rights Reserved.

IN THE Corner

FINANCE 22
BUSINESS 23
HEALTH & WELLNESS 62
MENTAL HEALTH 62
FAITH & INSPIRATION 62
FASHION 63
KIDPRENUER 63

MEET THE EDITORS — **03.**
Dr. Ashley Little - Editor In Chief
Dr. Jessica Mosley - Asst. Editor in Chief

ABOUT OUR EDITOR — **04.**
Meet Dr. Ashley Little

HERstory — **18.**
Dr. Vicki Irvin

HIDDEN FIGURE — **24.**
Lashawn Dreher

WOMEN ON THE MOVE — **36.**
Chef Michelle A. Roberts
Andromeda Raheem
Charlene Rhinehart
Cher'Don Reynolds
Evonya Easley
Sylvia High

AUTHOR ON THE RISE — **56.**
Airnecia Mills

FUTURE MILLENNIAL MILLIONAIRE — **58.**
Cheylaina Fultz

KIDPRENEUR — **64.**
Aminah Rose

ASHLEYLITTLEENTERPRISES.COM

COVER STORY

CHRISTY RUTHERFORD
WHY SHE'S WINNING

Written By: Gracia Collins Rich

Women's Leadership Expert, Christy Rutherford's, aim is to lead women into the future of entrepreneurship and financial freedom. She provides them with the resources to navigate workplace politics while creating self-awareness and confidence to ASK for the compensation they truly deserve. This former U. S. Coast Guard Commander and 5x #1 Amazon Best-selling author has assisted her clients in receiving more than $11 million dollars in salary raises during the pandemic. One of her resounding mottos is, "Before people are willing to invest in you, you must be willing to invest in yourself". Christy is well equipped to help you see the BEST in yourself. Christy's show, *Why She's Winning*, destroys the myths that women in leadership can't have it all. She explores the lives of successful women who share incredible stories of their dynamic full lives that change the narrative and reveal the beauty of being a woman in leadership.

Who is Christy Rutherford?

I'm a free spirit, unicorn rider, visionary, comedian, world's best Auntie, and someone who's on a quest to make the world a better place.

What do you feel is your life's mission?

My life's mission is to awaken leaders to the reality that there are infinite possibilities available to them. To awaken leaders to their purpose, assist them with reclaiming their dreams, and illuminate their path to living a life of total fulfillment, as opposed to just settling for a job and a check.

Short term, my goal is to get 10,000 women, $1 billion in salary raises by 2025. Right now we're at $11 million in salary raises in a pandemic, so we have a little ways to go, but we're going to close the gap really fast this year.

What is the definition of entrepreneurship?

It depends on if you're working for purpose or if you're working for profit (solely). Entrepreneurship can be the pathway to freedom, so you can express your hidden talents and unexpressed energy. You can live as your Highest and best self by unapologetically sharing your gifts with the world. For entrepreneurs working from a place of purpose and passion, God provides the provision for you rendering useful service.

Entrepreneurs working solely for money, without the passion, purpose or intent to make the world a better place… Well, they can also be highly profitable, and usually find other ways to quell the desire of their Inner Being. Which can lead to self-destructive behavior or confusion of why large amounts of money hasn't resulted in "happiness" or inner peace.

What is the future of the Entrepreneur?

The quest to become a highly profitable entrepreneur comes with tremendous sacrifices. TREMENDOUS. Being misunderstood, ostracized, criticized, not maintaining mental and physical health and missing time with family and friends.

It's not easy and it takes conscious effort to try to balance it all. However, studying great leaders and entrepreneurs for the past +100 years, this is not new. It's just a part of the journey. My hope is that entrepreneurs will understand the sacrifices early on and consciously put in work to mitigate some of the fallout that comes with it. It's possible, but it takes conscious effort.

Christy, please share with the readers why is peace the new currency?

I don't think peace is necessarily the "new currency." Peace has always been currency. Money is energy.

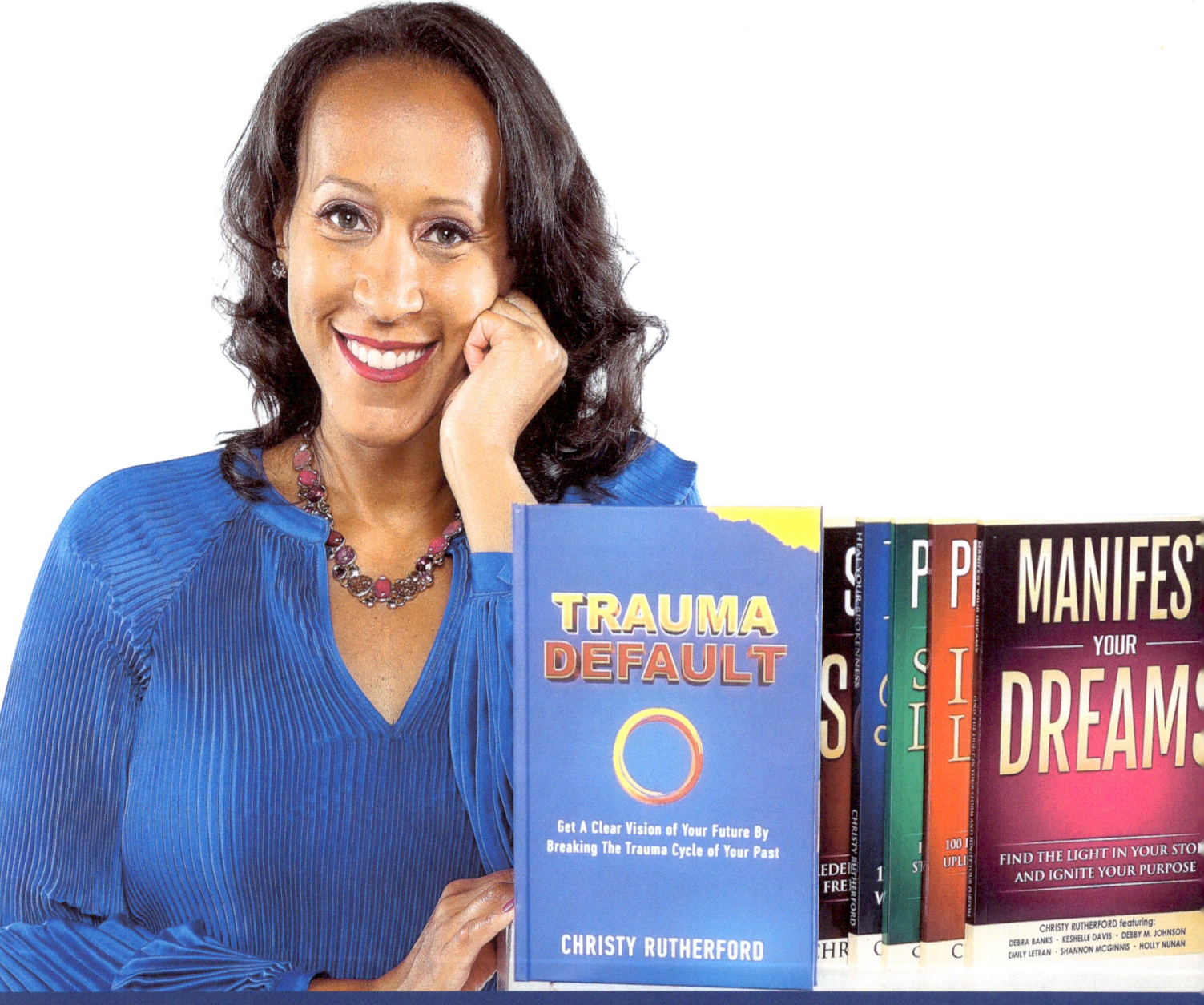

Money is currency. Attracting money is by energy, which is why they call money currency. If currents are connected and expressed with energy, then having more peace will allow more money to flow to you.

The challenge that I see in the world today is, people are giving up their peace, health, relationships, marriages, and family in the pursuit of money. Thinking that if they had money, they would have more peace. As opposed to understanding that if they had peace with themselves FIRST, they would be able to attract more money to them. Then, they would have a greater opportunity to use that money to make the world a better place, instead of just making themselves better.

So if people are solely chasing money as a means to have more peace, the "perfect" relationships or everything they want… well, they have it backwards.

Christy, please tell us more about your show *Why She's Winning*?

The goal with *Why She's Winning* is to create a new conversation with regards to what's possible for women in leadership. There are countless articles, studies, and stories that share women in leadership can't have it all. Or that we have to choose between a successful career and a marriage or children. Or being married with children, while trying to balance a career that it's normal and okay to operate at a deficit. Normalizing the conversation of being angry, stressed out, burned out, high-functioning anxiety and high-functioning depressed. These beliefs are UNTRUE and keeps women in toxic work environments, underpaid, underappreciated, undervalued, underemployed, but overworked. Women deserve better than that.
Since burning out and leaving my highly successful career with 3.5 years left to retire with a full pension, I had to learn the hard way that I should have managed my stress for the first 15 or so years in my career so I wouldn't have collapsed when I finally earned my seat at the table.

After working endlessly and checking all the boxes, we deserve to live a higher quality of life, but we're trapped in a detrimental cycle that we don't know how to break. After coaching hundreds of women to higher levels of success. Reclaiming their inner peace, quality time with family and restoring their mental and physical health, it's time to share those stories and we do that on my podcast.

We've saved over 25 marriages. Stopped 10 women from dying or having nervous breakdowns and kept hundreds of kids out of therapies from talking about their mommas. We've gotten +10 women off of high blood pressure medication and one of my clients completely healed from having fibroids and endometriosis in four months.

In addition, we've doubled 18 women's salaries and tripled nine. Four women got seven-figure packages, and over 20 women received at least a 30% salary raise at their jobs.

The goal is to share this insight and create a new narrative on what's possible with women in leadership. As opposed to reading the articles that always talks about how women are limited. I want to let women know that their opportunities are LIMITLESS.

It's Women's History Month, what woman in history or woman making history would you like for us to celebrate that's made an impact on your life or somehow inspired you?

The one woman that I would like to thank one day personally is Oprah. For the first 7 12 years of my career, I worked 80 hours a week, checked all the right boxes, went to all the Christmas parties, laughed at the jokes that weren't funny and sacrificed everything in my life to be able to create success in my career.

I started watching Oprah in 2009, and she completely shifted my way of thinking. Bringing me back from the separation that I had with my Inner Being and God. The amazing thought leaders she interviewed. like Wayne Dyer, Gary Zukav, Eckhart Tolle and Louise Hay who shared their insight around metaphysics, purpose and the Law of Attraction. I started my journey of spiritual development and a lot of personal development. And so, she introduced me to a lot of people that awakened me to the reality that my world could be greater and that my purpose was greater than just checking boxes at an amazing career that I built. Sensing my Inner Being stirring around in me and tapping into my inner core and bringing out the person that was WAITING to be unleashed to create significant change in the world.

Christy, please tell readers about your upcoming projects and how they can support.

I host monthly virtual events called "How to Calculate Your Value in the Market where I share how women in leadership can get a $50,000 raise in the next 90 days. Readers can register at no cost a LevelUpWithChristy.com.

I also have a free case study (25 minutes) that shares how women in leadership can get a 30% raise in 2023 without getting another degree. They can get that at ChangeNowWithChristy.com.

Please tell readers how they can follow you and support you on all social media platforms.

I'd love to connect with readers on LinkedIn (search my name)
Instagram @Christy.Rutherford
YouTube @ChristyRutherford
Facebook @theVisionFinder7

ABOUT CHRISTY RUTHERFORD
With over 20 years of leadership experience, Christy is an international executive leadership coach and business advisor. She assists women with getting promoted through office politics and self-care.

A Harvard Business School Alumna, Christy is also a certified Executive Leadership Coach from Georgetown University and has been featured in Forbes three times. An author, Christy published five #1 best-selling books on Amazon in eight months.

Christy is the 13th African American woman to achieve the rank of Commander (Lieutenant Colonel equivalent) in the U.S. Coast Guard's 230+ year history where her demographic was .1%.

COVER STORY

MONEI SUTTON
Serial Entrepreneur

Written By: Dr. Ashley Little

Movie Director, Model, Entrepreneur, Radio Host and Former Miss Teen USA. Monei Sutton, is a modern Renaissance Woman. Hailing from Atlanta, Georgia, Monei brings her God-given talents to all ventures she embarks on. As a leader and Serial Entrepreneur, Monei states that being an entrepreneur allows individuals to capitalize on their skills while creating a future. A mother who is passionate about the state of our youth, Monei is also the driving force behind her non-profit, which focus on health, education, and well-being of children. Monei personifies the inspiring combination of divine purpose and self-determination culminating into brilliant success.

Who is Monei Sutton?

Monei Sutton is a native of Atlanta Georgia, she is an award-winning actress, radio personality, fashion model fashionista, film producer, film director and entrepreneur. Who in addition is a nominee for a Doctorate degree in Humanitarian studies. Also, Monei Sutton is a mother to three beautiful daughters Taylor, Semaja, and Shalonte. She is also a philanthropist in other words she gives so much to her community through her non-profit organization that she values and cherishes so much as part of her life's work.

What do you feel is your life's mission?

Her life's Mission is to ensure the following.
- To cater to the needy in her community as best as she can.
- To showcase the God-given talent that she has to the world with grace and class.
- To help cater to less fortunate children and help provide for their needs.
- To help motivate single moms with children since I'm a single mom myself.

Her main life mission is to live a Godly-driven life and to be light for others to see and be an inspiration for others.

What is the definition of Entrepreneurship?
A person who organizes and operates a business or business, taking on greater than normal financial risks to do so. An entrepreneur is also an individual who creates a new business, bearing most of the risks and enjoying most of the rewards. The process of setting up a business is known as entrepreneurship. The entrepreneur is commonly seen as an innovator, a source of new ideas, goods, services, and business/or procedures.

What is the future of the Entrepreneur?

Entrepreneurship is critically important in this new and changing world because it allows individuals to oversee their own destinies, capitalize on their skills, and feel motivated to create their own future. Future entrepreneurship will be defined by new solutions that work anywhere. Solutions independent of location, serviced by remote

COVER STORY | MONEI SUTTON P. 17

workers. Take healthcare, which has completely transformed in a short period of time. Society is now far more invested in telehealth, remote diaagnostics, and medical devices.

Monei, what is the future of Women in Media?

I believe women in media today are winning, women are now being recognized and appreciated more than ever. As a woman coming from the media, I am where I am today because of the media. Coming from the world star family with a platform of 29 million viewers I was able to tap into multiple outlets which secure my main role as an actress and other platforms.

Monei, why are you so passionate about the Entertainment Industry?

Simple, I'm tailor-made for this. Ever since I was a kid, I felt I had multiple personalities so you never know what you will get.

It's Women's History Month. What woman in history or woman making history would you like for us to celebrate that's made an impact on your life or somehow inspired you?

A woman I would like for us to celebrate is so dear to me her name is the late Precious Harris, The artist T. I's sister, she was such an inspiration to me and helped get me to get to where I am today as a philanthropist. Because of her, she inspired me to rename my non-profit after her. (PRECIOUS FOUNDATION KIDS FOUNDATION) the motto is "Changing one kid at a time."

Monei, please tell readers about your upcoming projects and how we can support.

Currently, I'm in production with new feature films called:

- "THE DISPUTE"
- FLIP THE SCRIPT
- UNDER HIS CONTROL
- 6 SHOTS

Please tell readers how they can follow and support you on all social media platforms.

IG @therealmoneisutton_
FB Monei Sutton
TW @therealmoneisutton
www.therealmoneisutton.com

ABOUT MONEI SUTTON

The birthright of Montanique Sutton, who everyone now knows as The One and Only, Monei Sutton is a native of Atlanta, Georgia; the city of opportunities! And truly, this pioneer represents her home very well. As not only does she reside in the city of opportunities but she provides them. Ms. Sutton is a woman of branding, confidence, and achieving. In similarity of most African American youth, Monei was raised in the Christian faith under the denomination of The Church of God In Christ (COGIC), in which it all started. Monei was a faithful member of her church choir every Sunday. This is where she learned of her gift of singing. Ladder on, she branched out by performing in her schools' talent shows and just playfully practicing in the mirror as interviewing herself as her own celebrity. Monei's ideology was clear at a young age, entertainment was her and she was entertainment. Please, don't pull out a camera, Monei is known to strike a pose... LIGHTS, CAMERA, ACTION, TAPE 2 MONEI SUTTON REVEALS

In her city of opportunities, Miss "Monei" was crowned Miss Teen USA at the age 16. At that point, she developed more than just a career but a direction of her purpose. This enlarged her territory so, that her title landed her gigs that only one could only the phantom. But truly Monei knew it was to come as her love for entertainment and relationship with God, she knew if she asked it was already done. At the age 19, Monei explored life in new ventures where Monei became a proud mother at the age 19. Unlike others, she didn't allow motherhood hinder her achievements but to enhance it. Deeper than ever Monei use what she had and made it work for her and her daughter.

Today, you can find Monei Sutton, now known as Ms. Curvalicious in the areas of motherhood, print and runway modeling, hosting her own radio show, acting in films and most of all trusting God in all that she does. You didn't think we would give you all the details of Monei Sutton. No, continue to follow Monei as in all bookings, you will always learn something new about Monei Sutton.

*HER*story

Dr. Vicki Irvin

By: Gracia Collins Rich

Dr. Vicki Irvin is a SUPERWOMAN building her business on the 3B System (Business, Beauty and Balance). Dr. Irvin makes it a priority that women take care of themselves while taking care of business. A renowned business coach and marketing expert, Dr. Irvin has guided thousands of female entrepreneurs on the path of creating successful, profitable companies bringing in revenue of six and seven figures. She believes there is something inside each of us that inspires and is admired by others. It is our inner power, strength, and uniqueness that makes us powerful. Dr. Irvin encourages and coaches women on how to channel their power in both their businesses and personal lives to live in greater health and abundance.

Who is Dr. Vicki Irvin?

I have been a full-time entrepreneur for 17 years while juggling family life and my career. I have been teaching business owners how to create six and seven figure businesses by becoming marketing experts. More importantly, I am all about empowering women to care less about what other people think and to be intentional and unapologetic about what they want, a valuable lesson I too had to grasp.

Please tell us what being a business owner means to you and why you became an entrepreneur in the first place?

Being a business owner means you are a risk taker who believes you have something of value to offer your market and that nobody can execute that vision better than you. I became an entrepreneur after being exposed to other people making money doing something they loved. Watching them enjoy being the driver of their own destiny, changing lives and profiting at the same time was all I needed to see. I wanted in!

What has been your greatest influence in business and why?

My greatest influence in business has been watching the journey of other black women entrepreneurs from all different industries create wealth and legacy. Black women inherently have a lot of drive and desire to create something greater than themselves and that fuels and motivates me.

What are three different strategies you would like to share with small business owners to increase their bottom line?

Stay consistent. The majority of the money in your business will come from your ability to perform tasks in your business that may not be the most fun but will drive the most profits. The mundane things like building your list and following and staying in front of them is how you win.

Make sure what you are selling, and offering is fulfilling a need in the market that may be missing and be sure you know how to message it correctly so that it resonates with the right people who will be your buyers.

When it's time to scale up, make sure you are ready by reevaluating your team. As your profits increase, it may be time to get with people more experienced in your income bracket who know how to take you to the next level without sabotaging your business.

What does Women's History month mean to you?

It's a time of recognition and celebration to highlight the many accomplishments of women that have been historically overlooked or minimized. Women are doing phenomenal things across all industries in a world where we are not always given credit. As we strive to be on equal footing with men, taking the time to remind the world that we are the backbone of society is always extremely important.

What upcoming projects do you have coming up?

My health and wellness/supplement line Black Woman Lifestyle is expanding into merchandise and clothing, as well as the rebranding of my SWL Cosmetics line to Black Woman Lifestyle Cosmetics. These are two projects we will be rolling out in the next few months that I'm extremely excited about.

Please tell readers how they can follow and support you on all social media platforms?

I can be followed and supported at: @vickiirvin across all social media platforms.

ASHLEYLITTLEENTERPRISES.COM

*HER*story

HERstory | DR. VICKI IRVIN

ABOUT DR. VICKI IRVIN

Dr. Vicki Irvin is a marketing expert who has coached thousands of women entrepreneurs and celebrities on how to start and grow successful six and seven figure businesses over the last 15 years. Part of her movement has always included showing women just how important it is to be in the best physical shape they can be, and so she created the Black Woman Lifestyle brand. Health and wealth go together and Vicki is now on a concerted effort to show more women of color how to live their best life through her supplement line created specifically for black women, on-line community, and wellness coaching.

For over 15 years, her widely recognized annual three-day Extreme Women Entrepreneurs Event has hosted women entrepreneurs and business owners from all over the world who come to learn what's new and working in the areas of marketing and sales conversion to acquire more customers. Black Enterprise magazine recently tapped Vicki for her top tips and strategies on executing successful and profitable events, conferences and seminars. Vicki is a frequent host and correspondent for red carpet events and appearances and has covered the BET Honors, BET Bobby Jones Gospel and Bally's Las Vegas.

In 2013 Vicki entered the ecommerce space within the beauty industry and became the creator and founder of the SWL Cosmetics Collection, a full-service cosmetics company and line that is sold world-wide and caters to women of color.

Vicki has been featured in such medias as Millionaire Blueprint Magazine, Essence Magazine, CNN News, USA Today, Lifetime TV, Bloomberg Radio, Black Enterprise, Essence.com, and Investor's Business Daily. Vicki is the author of "The Superwoman Lifestyle Blueprint." "The Secret Diary of a Superwoman" and the "Superwoman Lifestyle Brand Building Blueprint" all of which are available on Amazon.

Vicki holds a Master's Degree in Human Resource Development and was awarded an Honorary Doctorate of Philosophy.

ASHLEYLITTLEENTERPRISES.COM

FINANCE CORNER

EMPLOYMENT TAXES – WHAT ARE THEY AND WHAT HAPPENS IF YOU FAIL TO PAY

Written By: Dr. Cozette M. White

If you have employees, you are responsible for paying a variety of taxes at the federal, state, and local levels. You must also withhold certain taxes from the paychecks of your employees. So, what are employment taxes?

Employment taxes include the following:

- Federal income tax withholding
- Social Security and Medicare taxes
- Federal unemployment tax (FUTA)

Federal Income Taxes/Social Security and Medicare Taxes

You generally must withhold federal income tax from wages paid to an employee. Form W-4 is used to determine the specific amount, although most payroll services or your accountant will do this for you.

Social security and Medicare taxes pay for benefits that workers and families receive under the Federal Insurance Contributions Act (FICA). Social security tax pays for benefits for the retired, survivors, and disability insurance distribution provisions of FICA. Medicare tax pays for benefits under the medical care provisions of FICA. As an employer, you must withhold a percentage of these taxes from employee and match the withholding amount.

In general, you must deposit these taxes by check or cash, to an authorized financial institution, typically your bank. Check with your tax professional to make sure you are not required to use the Electronic Federal Tax Deposit System (EFTPS). Regardless of the payment method, you will then report them on Form 941, the Employer's Quarterly Federal Tax Return.

Federal Unemployment Tax (FUTA)

FUTA is a combined federal and state program that provides unemployment compensation to the unemployed. As a business owner, you are solely responsible for paying this tax; to wit, nothing is withheld from the paychecks of your employees. FUTA is determined by using Form 940, but you are encouraged to use a tax professional to determine payment amounts.

Employment taxes can be frustrating for a small business owner. They are, unfortunately, a necessary evil as your business grows.

As an employer, you must pay employment taxes if you have employees. Fail to pay and the IRS will rain all over your parade.

Penalties

If you have employees, you absolutely must deduct and withhold various taxes from the paychecks of your employees. Since you are deducting money from the employee's paycheck, you are handling their funds. This fact is very important to the IRS and it places great emphasis on any failure to deposit employment taxes.

If you fail to pay employment taxes, you will be subject to a 100 percent penalty. Yes, 100 percent. Known as the "trust fund recovery penalty," the penalty is assessed against the person responsible for paying the taxes, not the entity. The person can be the owner, corporate officer or other "responsible person." In short, a business entity is not going to protect you from the wrath of the IRS.

Late Payments

Cash flow crunches are an inevitable event for practically every business. So, what happens if you make a late payment for employment taxes. Unless you can show a reasonable reason for the delay, the IRS is going to penalize you.

Late payment penalties range in amount depending on the delay. We may charge penalties if you do not make required deposits on time, make deposits for less than the required amount or if you do not use EFTPS when required. We will not charge penalties if you did not willfully neglect to make a proper and timely deposit and you have a reasonable cause.

For amounts not properly or timely deposited, the penalty rates are:

2% — deposits made 1 to 5 days late;

5% — deposits made 6 to 15 days late;

10% — deposits made 16 days or more late, but on or before the 10th day after the date of the first notice we sent you asking for the tax you owe;

10% — deposits made to an unauthorized financial institution, or payments made directly to the IRS, or paid with your tax return;

10% — Amounts subject to electronic deposit requirements but not deposited using EFTPS;

15% — Amounts still unpaid more than 10 days after the date of the first notice the IRS sent asking for the tax due or the day on which you receive notice and demand for immediate payment, whichever is earlier.

In Closing

Whatever you do, make sure you deposit employment taxes with the IRS in a timely fashion. Take a moment to think about the worst thing you have ever heard done by the IRS. If you fail to pay employment taxes, the actions taken by the IRS will be ten times worse and you will be the one telling horror stories.

More on Dr. Cozette M. White

Dr. Cozette M. White helps tax and accounting professional start and grow highly profitable virtual firms. She is an acclaimed best-selling author, nationally recognized finance and tax strategist, international speaker and philanthropist.

Dr. Cozette is the resident Money Matters Expert for Fox40. Dr. Cozette is a two time awardee of the Presidential Lifetime Achievement Award by President Barack Obama and President Joseph Biden.

Read more about Cozette and the services offered via her website http://www.MyFinancialHome.com. Follow Dr. Cozette on LinkedIn and other platforms @cozettemwhite

FINANCE & BUSINESS CORNER

WHAT DO WE DO NEXT?

Written By: Nykole Wyatt

We have seen the real estate market move up and down more so in the last two years than in any other time in history. There has been talk of a crash happening. There are experts that say a crash won't happen. The one thing that I can say for sure is pay attention to interest rates. Interest rates are always a key indicator of how the real estate market will function. When interest rates were low, buyers flocked into the market which created an imbalance between buyers and sellers. The imbalance was so great you saw buyers virtually giving their lives away just to have a home. Once interest rates began to go up, buyers began to pull out of the market and homes began to sit. Only savvy buyers knew to take advantage of rising interest rates. I mean Dave Ramsey said it best, "This is the best time to buy a home in the next five years." Now that we know this useful piece of information, what do we do next? How do we navigate the ups and downs? First thing is first, get your mind right. Too many of you are running scared. Man up, woman up and get what God has for you. Contact an expert in the industry and make your next real estate move. Scared money does not make money and scared money won't get you a real estate property. Get the knowledge you need to move forward. Explore the options available because in most states the market is not going to get back to the days we experienced with the mortgage crash of 2007 and 2008.

Buy the house. Buy the property. Get it now while you still have a chance. Don't let fear, obstacles and even judgment stop you. It's 2023 and this is your year!

RAISING YOUR PERSONAL STANDARDS IN 2023:

Written By: Everold Reid

Every year since I can remember I hear many friends, family members and colleagues talk about personal new years resolutions, bigger goals, and great aspirations. "This is the year," some say. I have said that a time or two and can relate especially when it comes to loosing a few pounds.

These are all great goals to talk about as many people correlate a fresh start with a brand-new year. Many will set massive goals, discuss a plan of action, and even start, but by this time of the year the cracks in the master plan become prevalent.

Let's talk about a Success plan that works. Our habits decide our lives so its important to understand the "consciousness of our habits". What we think we do habitually vs. what we do.

Motivation: This is an area where many people faulter from the get-go. It's important to know what drives you, what excites you and what gives you the most peace of mind. Write these things down as part of your success plan.

Focus: Get rid of the distractions! Social media and TV are among the worst distractions that ceases your valuable time away from your Success plan. The glamor and bling you often see others share is not their reality either and if they had a massive success plan, they wouldn't waist time posting about their last meal.

Confidence: is about knowing who we are and that we can become more capable. Confidence drives you to seek the information from wherever it may be and to seek opinions even when they differ. Instead of questioning yourself, ask that question or share that idea in the meeting.

Energy: Raising your personal standards to achieve your life goals starts with your inner self. You must commit to taking care of you! Your overall strategy should include a healthy lifestyle including diet, exercise, and meditation even if it's minimum five minutes each day. The key here is consistency in this discipline to develop the mental and physical strength required to work on your success plan.

Purpose: Purpose driven individuals always have a way of thriving and becoming high achievers because they find a way no matter what to navigate to their goal. When your goals are purpose driven you are pulled towards high achievement instead of dispensing valuable energy of pushing your way through.

Execute: This is where the rubber meets the road. Having a lavish plan, neatly documented goals won't do much for your success unless you Execute! Too many people fail here at this most important discipline because they allow distractions or fear of failure to slow them down. Executing your plan is where you learn and grow as you make mistakes, redo, and learn some more.

#BeIntentional #BeEmpathetic #ListenMore #AddValue #Communicate

www.linkedin.com/in/everoldreid/
www.thereidmethod.com/
www.yaandy.com

ASHLEYLITTLEENTERPRISES.COM

HIDDEN FIGURE

Lashawn Dreher

By: Kirby Wilson

Media Maven, Lashawn Dreher shares stories of Black women with the World. As Founder of BlkWomenHustle® and Editor-In-Chief of *EMOIR Magazine*, she created a niche that has allowed her to partner with many of the most impressive companies such as ESSENCE and Meetup. As a marketing strategist and digital brand creator, Lashawn has developed a formidable formula for success that she shares with her community of black female entrepreneurs. It is important to her how the narratives of Black women entrepreneurs are shared, and she empowers them through her workshops on marketing trends and monetizing digital content. Lashawn feels that now is the time to honor Black women and their world changing contributions, and it is her goal to do so through her dynamic platforms.

Who is Lashawn Dreher?

Outside of the business, I'm just a mother and a woman who loves to lay low, catch a vibe, and build with my people.

Please tell us what being a business owner means to you and why you became an entrepreneur in the first place?

I always knew I wanted to be an entrepreneur, but never really understood the depth of the role until I was in it. Being an entrepreneur wasn't in my plans, it landed during a time of hardship and being left with the choice of "sink or swim", with a child in tow. But here I am over 5 years later, constantly learning what it takes to truly be successful as a business owner. Being in this position means more than making money. The work we do, along with the services and products we provide are enhancing someone's life. The mission is what means the most.

What has been your greatest influence in business and why?

Black Women and our past and current struggles remain one of my greatest business influences. I'm always honored to say that I celebrate, support, and build businesses for Black Women for a living. I know what it's like to endure the misogyny, racism, and disrespect that comes with being in our skin. So, working to combat each of those things will always be a driving force behind my business.

What are three different strategies you would like to share with small business owners to increase their bottom line?

Apply the knowledge you've obtained before you overconsume. It's possible to take multiple courses, get degrees, or read books, and still be clueless when it comes to making money. Take the time to implement what you've learned and let the knowledge work for you. That's where you'll find the revenue you're looking for. Hire an accountant to organize your finances. Many entrepreneurs go into business thinking I'm making the money, so I'll just pay myself. That revenue is not the same as profit. Some of that

HIDDEN FIGURE | LASHAWN DREHER

money should be allocated to cover operations to keep the business afloat. Losing track of these line items will land you in the red. Make sure you're getting paid, but don't forget to actually make a profit.

Don't try to do everything and start small. Take your time to build your revenue and scale the business after. Focus on the products with the highest demand or services you provide with an elite level of expertise. When customers see that what you have to offer is THE product or service to have, it'll increase the likelihood of interest and engagement. And with a solid strategy and funnel, those leads eventually turn into conversions.

Why are you so passionate about media and sharing black women stories?

I always think back to the adolescent and adult years of seeing the magazine stands or watching different new channels and recounting the feeling of being absent. There were no women who looked like me. There weren't stories being told that resonated with the lifestyle of a Black girl or woman. And if they were told, it rarely felt authentic, as if someone else changed our words to fit their narrative of us. If Black Women were pictured, I always knew it could be better, that we could be seen and appreciated for more than just our beautiful curves and distinct features.

I wanted to see our stories told in truth, without shrinking, without stereotypes or being viewed as a monolith. It was imperative to make that change as soon as I had the ability to, so I did. Black Women are the blueprint, we create the trends, we're versatile, and our culture is one of one. We deserve to tell our stories with that at the forefront.

Where do you see Black Women in the media in five years?

I see us stepping into roles that allow us to take control of our narratives and the stories of our people in general. This past year, I've seen so many Black Women journalists, editors, and content creators becoming more vocal about who's telling our stories and how. We've often been silenced while others have allowed inaccuracies and white washing to fly, and it seems many of us have come to a point of making sure it doesn't happen again.

What does Women's History month mean to you?

This is what I call the most beautiful time of the year. Women are positioned in a spotlight that doesn't often get shined on us from others. The women I've met and built relationships with, the platforms created, the women within the networks built by Black Women, they all celebrate our historic strides each day. So, it's a normal occurrence for us, but we're still honored to share their accomplishments with the world to let them see what they've been missing. There are countless women many of us know who've made history, but they've gone without the national headlines and recognition. This is the time in which they get to receive their flowers and honors for changing the world.

What does Hidden Figures mean to you?

Hidden Figures are the doers. They've been silent on the social scene, but the work is always being done. Their impact is immeasurable, they're well-known, but you don't hear nor see their names in the media often. But they're the true heroes that keep many people and businesses thriving. You might not realize it, but they're the people you need to know!

What upcoming projects do you have coming up?

All I can tell you is that the BlkWomenHustle and EMOIR Magazine collaborations for 2023 are going to change more lives and businesses for Black Women.

Please tell readers how they can follow and support you on all social media platforms?

Lashawn Dreher
Site: lashawndreher.com
IG: @lashawndreher
Twitter: @lashawndreher
LinkedIn: Lashawn Dreher, MBA
https://www.linkedin.com/in/lashawn-dreher-mba

BlkWomenHustle
Site: blkwomenhustle.com
IG: @blkwomenhustle
Facebook: Blk Women Hustle
https://www.facebook.com/blkwomenhustle/
Twitter: @blkwomenhustle1
LinkedIn: BlkWomenHustle
https://www.linkedin.com/company/blkwomenhustle

EMOIR Magazine
Site: emoirmagazine.com
IG: @emoirmagazine
Facebook: EMOIR Magazine
https://www.facebook.com/emoirmagazine
Twitter: @emoirmagazine
LinkedIn: EMOIR Magazine
https://www.linkedin.com/company/emoir-magazine

ABOUT LASHAWN DREHER

Lashawn Dreher is the Founder of BlkWomenHustle®, Editor-in-Chief of EMOIR Magazine, and powerhouse Marketing Strategist amplifying Black Women's voices and businesses. She has facilitated workshops for thousands of Black Women entrepreneurs, educating them on evolving marketing strategies, curating memorable content, digital monetization, and effectively building social capital.

Working with prominent clients, she has expanded audiences, curated nationwide events, tours, content, and campaigns, and organized partnerships with companies, including ESSENCE, The Sistahs in Business Expo, Meetup, and Thinkific. She's grown digital audiences of 300,000+ for multiple women's platforms, increasing engagement, revenue, and enhancing their online experiences.

She emerged as the Networking Maven™ when launching BlkWomenHustle®— the global, all-in-one networking platform for a collective 110k+ Black Women entrepreneurs, professionals, and creatives. With every connection, women are positioned to network with purpose, learn from industry-leading experts, and grow profitable businesses. The platform's annual list of Black Women Entrepreneurs to Watch has garnered the interest of thousands and become a primary resource for individuals and corporations looking to partner and connect with Black Women. Honorees listed have been presented with media and partnership opportunities with companies like McDonalds and ESSENCE. Through intentional events, collaborative spaces, profit-building resources and opportunities, and an impactful podcast, BlkWomenHustle ® has become the go-to platform positioning Black Women to become the most sought-after and highest paid.

Lashawn expanded her territory as a journalist, hosting and interviewing some of the world's most innovative and influential black women entrepreneurs on The BlkWomenHustle ® Podcast. In April 2022, she launched EMOIR Magazine, the newest digital media company and interactive publication celebrating the ventures and success of enterprising Black Women. Its contents address the multitude of civic and cultural topics relative to their personal and professional lifestyles.

Her notable features include recognition as a Gender Equality Innovator by Ticket Tailor and Women's History Month honors by Rolling Out. Lashawn's energetic persona motivates Black Women to show up authentically to take action and authority over their lives. Her passion remains rooted in creating the spaces and opportunities they deserve to continuously make groundbreaking moves in business.

MILLION DOLLAR MOGULS

Jasmine Womack

By Dr. Cozette M. White

She has a an affinity for books. She reads them, writes them and also helps other business owners and executives craft their work of art into a 7-Figure Online Business. Meet Jasmine Womack, CEO and Founder of E.M.P.A.C.T. Group.

Jasmine you are the CEO/Founder of The E.M.P.A.C.T. Group please tell the readers more about your company?

The E.M.P.A.C.T. Group provides the following support, including but not limited to:

- Executive Coaching
- Educational Consulting & Training with Staff and Leadership Teams
- Business Coaching for Authors and Entrepreneurs
- Writing Coaching for Leaders and Experts
- Workshops, Presentations (Virtual In-Person), Speaking

I've been empowering through the pen and the spoken word to influence and transform lives for nearly 20 years. It's my life's mission and calling to work with high performing leaders and entrepreneurs to help you increase your sense of personal fulfillment and discover your true purpose by impacting the world.

Share with the readers how you were able to successfully grow your firm.

I grew my business by going live consistently a minimum of one time each week for one year, and connecting with others who had audiences of my ideal client. I also fine-tuned my messaging and became extremely specific with who I was targeting. Over time, I began to invest in sponsorships and paid advertising.

More than anything, I made sure to always provide my clients with a superior experience and great customer service. This usually got us great testimonials and referrals.

What are three different strategies you would like to share with small business owners to increase their bottom line?

1. Watch your spending.

2. Be mindful of your rates and ensure that the rates you are charging will cover your expenses and yield a profit.

ASHLEYLITTLEENTERPRISES.COM

MILLION DOLLAR MOGULS

3. Invest in coaching or high-level mentorship and implement the strategies into your business. You don't know what you don't know and, in my opinion, free resources will only take you so far. The best of the best always has an amazing coach.

How did you grow your viewers?

Collaborations - connecting with others, sharing platforms

Speaking and Podcasts - one of the easiest ways to increase your viewership is to connect with others who already have an audience of your ideal clients and speak to them. This can be done both in person and virtually.

Paid Advertising - Paid advertisement finds the people for you so that you don't have to manually do everything.

What are some strategies you would give to Entrepreneurs who are looking to grow and launch their products on national platforms?

Hire a publicist or dedicate the time and space to become your own publicist.

Make sure that your "back end" is set up appropriately. I often find that entrepreneurs want the "shine" and the "public eye," but don't invest in the proper infrastructure to handle the traffic it and when it comes. Have your lead magnets, conversions products and email systems established and set up.

What or who has been your greatest influence in business and why?

I don't have a particular business influence; however, I love reading rags to riches stories and books about Black Americans who defied the odds and became successful.

Are there any resources or tools you'd like to share with other small business owners that have helped you run your business? If yes, please describe (and include links if available).

- Kajabi - All in one system that operates your entire online business
- Dubsado - Customizable CRM
- Copy.ai - I'm still trying this out but I absolutely love copy.ai. I am able to take transcriptions of live streams or different notes and copy.ai will create captions and more from my content.
- Otter - Transcribe your notes

Do you have any new projects coming up (or have you just completed a big project ≈ reached a milestone, etc.)? If so, please tell us about it:

Yes! My annual event, Published and Paid Live (formerly Six Figure Storyteller Live) which will be held in Atlanta, GA October 27-29, 2023. This is the ONLY Three Day Event Designed to Help Experts Elevate Your Authority, Write a Best Selling Book, and Transform Your Book Into a 7-Figure Online Course and Coaching Business. www.publishedandpaidlive.com

What do you do for fun/relaxation?

Traveling, roller skating, and spending time with my family

Is there anything else you'd like to share with our readers?

Proverbs 16:3: Commit to the Lord whatever you do, and He will establish your plans

Please tell readers how they can follow and support your on all social media platforms?

www.jasminewomack.com
www.linkedin.com/in/thejasminewomack
www.youtube.com/@thejasminewomack
instagram.com/thejasminewomack
TikToc: thejasminewomack

MILLION DOLLAR MOGULS

Dee Edwards Fomby

By Dr. Cozette M. White

If Faith Had Its Way, It Would Have Selected Dee Edwards Fomby!
This dynamic millionaire shares her story to riches and her new venture.

You are the CEO/Founder of Dee Edwards Fomby please tell the readers more about your company?

Hey y'all, I am Dee Edwards Fomby, the brand. I find out what people need, and I create services and products to meet their needs depending on profit margins and my ability to execute in excellence. I am the founder of Tax Genie Tax Services & Professional Software, IRS Tax Academy, Snow White Tooth Solutions, Prophetic Street Gear, Dee Fomby Coaching & Consulting Services, and I am the co-founder of Roadrunner Slingshot Rentals, Resource Realty, WB40 Real Estate LLC, and The Link Entrepreneur Center.

Share with the readers how you were able to successfully grow your firm.

I was able to successfully build several profitable and sustainable brands through consistency, coaching, and healing of the soul. I knew that I wanted to make an impact in the world, therefore, I found the industry that I could find purpose and help others; then I discovered how I could enhance it and be the difference maker without recreating the wheel, and I showed up. I believe that many people don't show up consistently with their time and message in their business due to brokenness and soul trauma. What isn't healed shows up the most even in business or prevent most people from operating fully in their purpose.

What are three different strategies you would like to share with small business owners to increase their bottom line?

The three different strategies I suggest to help small business owners increase their bottom line are: discover your niche to build your audience. When working in a broad area like the tax industry, to stand out, you must be known for something in that industry specifically. I highly suggest becoming very knowledgeable in the niche to draw others and use it to attract clients interested in your products and services. And when you do, you will discover how to create messaging and marketing around your audience to attract more paying customers to your business. When you attempt to sell to everyone, you sell to no one. When you understand your audience, you can develop a message that will attract the right audience through various marketing strategies. I also suggest understanding trends and figuring out a way to include them in your brand without compromising the value while remaining relevant. In today's society, reels and TikTok's are trending, and most platforms provide selling opportunities of your products and services while expanding your reach. Lastly, I would suggest that

ASHLEYLITTLEENTERPRISES.COM

small business owners understand their revenue plan. A revenue plan is a breakdown of products and services, cost, and how many of each are needed to be sold to reach their revenue goal. When they understand this, they will understand which products are low-hanging fruit, and/or high-ticket items, and how many are needed to be sold to reach their profit margin. I find that many entrepreneurs, don't know their number.

How did you grow your viewers?

I grew my audience by simply showing up. Over a year ago, I went through a divorce and experience multiple death including my mom, and I still showed up consistently. It was easy for me to do so because when you operate in purpose, it has the ability to reach back and heal you. The LORD told me if I heal his people, He would heal me in the process. While I was going through my healing process, I continued to operate in purpose that brought healing to my soul. I found out that self-care is important, but stopping during the wrong season can kill the visionary.

What are some strategies you would give to Entrepreneurs who are looking to grow and launch their products on national platforms?

In order to grow or launch their products on national platforms, be faithful over little and you will be made ruler over much. Be faithful by being consistent, presentable, innovative, and authentic. I suggest becoming an author around your brand. It helps you with becoming a thought leader and your expertise can be showcased.

What or who has been your greatest influence in business and why?

If I can be honest, I would say myself. I am a little country girl that come from humble beginnings. In spite of hardships and many failures, I have been able to overcome them all, and accomplish and achieve success in ministry and marketplace. I grew up as a troubled child. I was the one that caused my mother many sleepless nights, but by the age of 20 I had purchased my first home and now I am the owner of residential and commercial properties. I have a long way to go, and my vision continues to grow, but when I sit down and think about it, I am so proud of myself. Nobody knows your story like you, so you deserve to clap the loudest for you in humility and grace.

Are there any resources or tools you'd like to share with other small business owners that have helped you run your business? If yes, please describe.

Since we are living in a day and age where social media is the trend, it is important for me to have simple, go to apps and websites to help with building my brand. I recommend the following:

- Canva for flyers, presentation, and social media graphics.
- Fiverr for just about any and everything for a small business owner.
- Capcut for editing of reels.
- Kajabi for email marketing, course creation, community, subscriptions, and product sales.

Do you have any new projects coming up (or have you just completed a big project ~ reached a milestone, etc.)? If so, please tell us about it:

Yes, my beautiful and amazing husband, Jeremiah and I are building out a 6000 square feet entrepreneur center in Birmingham called The Link. The vision is to link those in ministry to the marketplace with resources, workshops, seminars, tools, and strategies to be successful in business. We are set to open by June 2023. In addition, I recently released a brand-new book, CEOs, Pray Too, 31-days to building your business God's way. It provides scriptures, wisdom, and guidance to those who desire to build a business successful without compromising their faith and belief.

What do you do for fun/relaxation?

I love spending time with my family, friends and traveling. My husband and I spend a lot of time traveling in ministry. We serve in ministry and lead in the marketplace. We believe you can be saved and paid at the same time.

Is there anything else you'd like to share with our readers?

I would like to share with the readers to focus on increasing your abilities. Matthew 25 say that each servant was given a bag of silver based upon their abilities. The 1st two servants knew how to increase what was given to them because of their abilities. The dictionary say that abilities mean power or capacity to do or act physically, mentally, legally, morally, financially, etc. Abilities are increased through knowledge, wisdom, experiences, and suffering. According to Biblical standards, to whom much is given even much more is required and you will only be trusted with more based upon your abilities and your faith.

Please tell readers how they can follow and support you on all social media platforms

I can be reached on:

Instagram @DeeFomby
Facebook @deeFombyMinistries
YouTube @deeFomby

PB
PAMELA BODLEY™

Interviewing Strategies for Teens
with Pamela Bodley

Text **"Workshop"** to **66866** for a short video on the program

A comprehensive, engaging "real talk" fun workshop facilitated by the creator, Pamela Bodley, speaker, published author, and entrepreneur. Students will learn characteristics and strategies for a successful interview, e.g., how to dress, when to show up, what to bring, how to research the company, resume, cover letters, thank you notes, integrity as an employee, how to answer the difficult interview questions and much more!

SERVING AGES 14-23

TO BOOK A WORKSHOP
CALL OR EMAIL:

Phone: 914-207-6000
E-mail: info@pamelabodley.com

Our Partners

FEATURE STORY

Women on the Move

CHEF MICHELLE ROBERTS

*Written By:
Gracia Collins Rich*

Chef Shell makes every meal feel like home. This Atlanta Culinary Queen, by way of Jacksonville, Florida brings dynamic flavor profiles to mouthwatering Southern favorites. Chef Shell believes that cooking brings the community together. There is an essence of family when we all gather for delicious food. Trained in international cuisine, Chef Shell's goal is to bring you an immersive experience every time. In 2023, she is continuing to expand her business offering virtual cooking classes, meal prep, and a private chef experience.

WOMEN ON THE MOVE

Who is Chef Michelle Roberts?

Chef Shell is a private chef, caterer, author, and mother to three beautiful adult children. Before pursuing a career in culinary arts, Chef Shell was a full time IT professional, reserving her grand cooking skills to cook for family, friends, and holidays for over thirty years. She has been featured in Authority Magazine, Shoutout Atlanta, Black Profits, and most recently brought her talent to the screen on "The Willie Mo Jr. Show". Chef Shell received her culinary degree from Escoffier School of Culinary Arts in 2022. There she was formally trained in Spanish, Asian, French, American, and a multitude of other cuisines! It is her goal to continuously offer her clients a unique dining experience by infusing flavors from all over the world.

Please tell us what being a business owner means to you and why you became an entrepreneur in the first place?

Being a business owner means no longer operating in fear. It's having the courage to step out on faith, with your God given talent, AND say "Here I am world, Here I am!". I have always had an entrepreneurial spirit. I've sold Mary Kay, I sell insurance, and a plethora of other ventures. I have a desire for financial freedom, and a desire to lead my family into generational wealth. I want to encourage other women like me, who had every reason to give up, but didn't!

What has been your greatest influence in business and why?

Lisa Brooks, a dynamic woman and chef helped me catapult my business forward and mentored me on price dynamics to make my Chef and catering services more profitable and to increase my overall growth potential. She definitely inspired me to keep pressing forward and come up with savvy ways to increase clientele.

What are three different strategies you would like to share with small business owners to increase their bottom line?

1. Know your Numbers (how much you spend on products, and how much you want to make) Be conscious of your profit margins!

2. Keep learning and growing. Engaging your audience through all Media outlets (Website, Email, Facebook, Instagram, Twitter, Pinterest, Snap Chat, TikTok, Clubhouse and any new digital outlets that will come)!

3. Know your audience (Client Avatar), know the demographic, the age, the needs and desires and then meet that need with your service, and excellence.

What does Women's History month mean to you?

It means empowering women, uplifting the community and advocating for lifelong learning. It is never too late to go after what you desire, and with commitment and perseverance anything can be achieved! I come from a strong lineage of women. This month I salute them, and all they have ingrained in my spirit, heart, and mind. I honor myself by serving and being a blessing to others.

What upcoming projects do you have coming up?

Valentine's Day Romantic Dinner (A private dining experience, or catering)

Food Tasting (An event that will showcase all Chef Shell's merchandise, include a select menu of some of my tastiest, soul -smacking recipes, and the opportunity to network with fellow black-owned businesses all over Atlanta)

Weekly Soul food Menu (Every Soul Food Friday I provide a select menu that includes a choice of an entree, two sides, and dessert)

Furthermore, as I begin to expand and increase, I will open a restaurant to serve up my delicious cuisines, and recipes! Changing lives just a little soul food at a time.

Please tell readers how they can follow and support you on all social media platforms?

www.drshellssoulfood.com
www.instagram.com/dr.shellskitchen
www.facebook.com/drshellsoulfood
www.pinterest.com/drshellskitchen/
www.youtube.com/watch?v=zbOX0c6qU8I
www.tiktok.com/dr.shellskitchen

ABOUT CHEF MICHELLE A. ROBERTS

Chef Shell's passion and love for my family and the people in my community, has encouraged me to bring joy to them through food and cooking. The recipes I have were given to me from my Granny Mary Lee Tyler, Aunt Gussie, and Grandma Penn. I was blessed to have such inspirational women in my life to pass on this great tradition with the world. I consider everyone who has Dr. Shells Soul Food Cooking friends and family, so I feel that I'm blessed to share my gifts with you all. I provide catering services, private chef services and weekly soul food delivery.

Michelle is an Atlanta native with 3 Adult Kids and one grandson who she adores. Michelle loves Atlanta and the community. She is an avid Falcons Fan and prides herself on women empowerment and community advocacy.

Working as an IT professional by day and a Soul Food Chef by night, Michelle loves to cook meals that truly bring people joy, warms their heart, and fills the soul. She has been cooking over 30 years with passion and soul.

ASHLEYLITTLEENTERPRISES.COM

ANDROMEDA RAHEEM

Written By:
Gracia Collins Rich

She Wins Society Founder, Andromeda Raheem, personal mantra is, when women support women, we all win. Andromeda is a Certified Master Life Coach and 2x published author. Andromeda left the constraints of corporate America behind to pursue her calling which is to create spaces for women of color and equip them to present their best selves through self-care and creative development services. Andromeda's focus is to create a sisterhood of women of color who are not only equipped to elevate in their personal and professional spaces, but to also create wealth for generations to come. She has many upcoming projects including the return of Stepping N2 Sisterhood later this month for the first time since the Pandemic.

WOMEN ON THE MOVE

Who is Andromeda Raheem?

Above all things, Andromeda Raheem is a woman who strives to be who God created her to be. She is a woman on a mission to fulfill her divine purpose and make a positive impact in the world. Her passion is creating spaces for women of color to attract and cultivate meaningful relationships, practice self-care, and develop a winning belief system so they can have the connections, capacity, and confidence needed to achieve goals, fulfill purpose, and make positive generational impact. Andromeda is a Certified Master Life Coach, 2x published author, and the Founder of She Wins Society. She wholeheartedly believes that there is greater power in unity and community and has consistently created opportunities for women of color to grow and win together since 2014. Her life's work is rooted in her personal mantra, *When women support women, we all win*. Andromeda's ultimate life goal is to leave an inspiring legacy that will positively impact women of color and their families.

Please tell us what being a business owner means to you and why you became an entrepreneur in the first place?

To me, being a business owner means contributing something of value to the world, creating products or services that make life easier for others, and solving problems in your community. I became an entrepreneur because I had a deep desire to fulfill my God-given purpose and create meaningful change in my community and the world. I earned my degree in accounting but found the work to be unfulfilling and out of alignment with what my spirit was calling for me to do. My search for my purpose led me to entrepreneurship because the vision God gave me for She Wins Society wasn't something that already existed. It was something I was inspired to build from the ground up.

What has been your greatest influence in business and why?

My greatest influence in business has been the belief that my life is not my own. I am here for a purpose that's bigger than my own feelings. Seeing my work transform the lives of others in real-time and hearing women tell me how much She Wins Society has helped them is what keeps me going in the midst of adversity. I am driven by the idea of leaving the world better than it was before I entered it and hearing God say, "job well done".

What are three different strategies you would like to share with small business owners to increase their bottom line?

The top three strategies that have been most beneficial to me in business are authenticity, consistency, and intentionality. Knowing who you are and being confident in who you are while consistently showing up in an impactful way and intentionally creating products, services, and content that serve the people who benefit most from your presence and gifts is the quickest way to build a community that will support you to grow your business. The more successful you are at attracting your tribe and assisting those people to get to a point where they feel like they know, like, and trust you, the more you will be able to scale your business and increase your bottom line.

Why are you so passionate about creating, empowering, providing resources, and opening doors for women globally?

I am so passionate about helping women access what they need to live healthy, happy, and in alignment with their purpose because I believe that the success of women makes a huge difference in the kind of world we live in. When a woman is her healthiest and happiest self, it impacts everyone and everything she is attached to. When she is empowered and equipped to make the best choices for her life, her relationships, household, children, work, and community all benefit. Women are the nurturers of the world. Every person living has to come through a woman. More happy and healthy women equate to a happier and healthier world.

What does Women's History month mean to you?

I love Women's History Month because it's a time when we get to see women intentionally celebrating other women. The energy during this month is always so amazing to experience. To me, Women's History Month means acknowledging the trails that have been blazed by the women who came before us and honoring women who are, in some way, making life better for other women and the world.

ASHLEYLITTLEENTERPRISES.COM

It's a special and designated month to take time to truly appreciate the power we have as women, the beauty in being a woman, and the accomplishments achieved by our sisters.

What upcoming projects do you have coming up?

I am so excited to announce that after a 3-year hiatus, Stepping N2 Sisterhood is finally back as an in-person event! Prior to the pandemic, She Wins Society hosted this networking and empowerment event in cities around the US each year. We pivoted to hosting it virtually for the last few years, but this year Stepping N2 Sisterhood will be hosted live in Orlando, Florida on Saturday, March 25, 2023! More information about this event and our 6th Annual Relax Relate Release Retreat can be found at shewinssociety.com.

Please tell readers how they can follow and support you on all social media platforms?

Please follow my work with She Wins Society on Instagram, Facebook, and Twitter @shewinssociety. You can also connect with me personally at @andromeda.wins on Instagram and Andromeda Raheem on Facebook.

ABOUT ANDROMEDA RAHEEM

Andromeda Raheem is a Certified Master Life Coach, 2x published author, motivational speaker, and the founder of She Wins Society, a social wellness centered organization that supports women of color to attract and cultivate meaningful relationships, practice self-care, and develop a winning belief system so they can have the connections, capacity, and confidence needed to achieve goals, fulfill purpose, and make positive generational impact. As Andromeda wholeheartedly believes that there is greater power in unity and community, she has dedicated the last 9 years of her life to creating spaces and opportunities for women to grow and win together. Her life's work is rooted in her personal mantra, *When women support women, we all win*. Andromeda has been featured in the Huffington Post, Sheen Magazine, Rolling Out, and on the Redefining Wealth Podcast, among many other reputable publications and platforms. Andromeda's ultimate life goal is to fulfill her divine purpose and leave an inspiring legacy that will positively impact current and future generations of women and their families.

ASHLEYLITTLEENTERPRISES.COM

CHARLENE RHINEHART

Written By:
Gracia Collins Rich

Investment Expert and Certified Public Accountant, Charlene Rhinehart teaches you how to put your money where the wealth is. As the Founder of Wealthy Women Daily, Charlene shares her knowledge of investing, banking, and creating lucrative portfolios with women looking to expand their financial horizons and achieve entrepreneurial goals. With almost two decades of experience in the accounting and finance arena, Charlene is a true mentor who uses her education and expertise to open doors for aspiring Black CPAs.

WOMEN ON THE MOVE

Who is Charlene Rhinehart?

Charlene Rhinehart is an award-winning Certified Public Accountant, author, and speaker based on Chicago's South Side. She is the founder of Wealthy Women Daily and the author of Dividends Are a Queen's Best Friend available on Amazon. She has served on the Financial Review Board for Investopedia and Chair of the Illinois CPA Society Individual Tax Committee. Charlene's financial insights have been published in national publications, including Black Enterprise, BlackDoctor.org, Essence Magazine, and AARP. She has spoke on many panels and conferences about the power of building a stock portfolio that's bigger than your shoe collection through dividend investing.

Please tell us what being a business owner means to you and why you became an entrepreneur in the first place?

Being a business owner means creating endless opportunities for the people in my community and around the world. It is my mission and duty to use my business to create the world that I would like to live in and spread a vision of financial freedom to those who may not think it's possible.

I became an entrepreneur because I didn't want to die with my gifts inside of me. In 2015, I won the title of Ms. Corporate America 2015. That moment changed the trajectory of my life and what was possible for me. I decided to leave my dream job in financial services to live my dream life. If the dream isn't powerful enough to propel you to action, hopefully the nightmare of never tapping into your potential will empower you to step into greatness.

I created a business so that I could have a platform to share my gifts with the world and help other women build a financial foundation so they could invest in their dream life. Imagine what more women could accomplish if money and time was not a problem. That vision drives the work that I do because I think the world would be a better place if people had more time to devote to the projects that align with their greater purpose.

What has been your greatest influence in business and why?

My mother inspired me to study accounting when I was in high school. After learning that accounting was the language of business, I knew that I wanted to become a Certified Public Accountant. Although there were stats floating around stating that less than 2% of CPAs were Black and that the CPA exam was more challenging than the BAR exam for lawyers, I knew the mission was greater than me. In 2010, I became a CPA while working in financial services.

As I progressed on my journey, I started studying the life of Mary T. Washington Wylie. In 1943, she became the first Black woman in the nation to earn the CPA license. What stood out the most for me was that Mrs. Washington Wylie opened her accounting firm on the South Side of Chicago and paved the way for future generations of accountants. During a time when black accountants couldn't gain access to mainstream jobs, she became a mentor, employer, and leader in the profession, allowing her firm to gain recognition as an "Underground Railroad" for aspiring Black CPAs. I am inspired to use my education to create the same opportunities for others.

When I was selected as one of 25 local journalists for a paid partnership with Meta's Bulletin platform, I created the Chicago Southsider newsletter which transitioned into a full website, www.ChicagoSouthsider.com, to tell the story of hidden business figures on the South Side of Chicago who had a national impact. Seeing what past generations have done in business influences my work and goals.

What are three different strategies you would like to share with small business owners to increase their bottom line?

Know your numbers. In order to achieve your business goals, you have to know your numbers inside and out. You should know where you are and where you want to go. Work with professionals like CPAs, financial planners, and tax advisors to help you understand your numbers and use them to make better business decisions. Having a clear understanding of financial statements is key to this process.

Master your craft. If you want to reach more people, you want to be known as the "go-to" person or resource for that specific product or service. Determine what you want to be known for and define your competitive advantage. Find out what your audience needs and become the solution they have been looking for. Put yourself in a position where you are so good at what you do that competition doesn't even exist.

Share your gifts. There is an audience that needs exactly what you have, but they probably don't know you exist yet. It's important to develop your media strategy so that you don't become the best kept secret. Develop your bio, create your media kit, and maintain your brand assets so that you can take advantage of opportunities when they knock on the door. The more people who know what you do, the more people you have a chance to impact.

ASHLEYLITTLEENTERPRISES.COM

WOMEN ON THE MOVE

Why are you so passionate about media and the finance industry?

Media is the microphone that allows people to gain access to information that can transform their lives. It controls what we do, how we behave, and who we aspire to become. If more people had access to good financial knowledge, they can make better decisions for themselves and their family.

The Road to Zero Wealth report published by Prosperity Now and the Institute for Policy Studies reveals that the median wealth of black Americans will fall to zero if current trends continue. I always tell people that their net worth is the sum of the decisions they have made. In our society, media influences many decisions. If we could transform the type of information that people are hungry for, then we can change the net worth and outcomes of many families around the world. Media gives us an opportunity to make strategic investments that can pay dividends over time.

What does Women's History month mean to you?

Women's History Month is a time to reflect on what's possible in our society by acknowledging the contributions women have made in various industries. But I don't confine my study of women's history to one month. I think it's important for women to understand the impact of women in society with every move we make. From starting impactful businesses to raising the next generation of leaders, women have played an influential role in the advancements we have made as people. When you know where you came from, you won't be confused about where you can go.

What upcoming projects do you have coming up?

I'm hosting a 5 Day Investing Challenge to help more women build a stock portfolio that's bigger than their shoe collection through dividend investing.

I also host Paychecks to Passive Income Masterclasses every month to help more women create their freedom portfolio from scratch and start their passive income journey through dividend investing.

For women who are mastering their financial goals and want to take their money knowledge to the next level, they can work with me through my Dividend Investing course. Students receive a course, workbook, and multiple 1:1 sessions with me to develop an income portfolio that pays them for the rest of their life.

When I'm not working with students, I'm delivering financial statement classes for corporate clients and hosting different financial shows such as Motley Fool's *The Path to Smarter, Happier, and Richer*. This year, I was a guest on CAN TV's In the Money show to discuss setting financial boundaries.

Please tell readers how they can follow and support you on all social media platforms?

You can follow me on the following social media platforms:

Charlene Rhinehart
Instagram: @charlenerhinehart
Facebook: Charlene D Rhinehart

Wealthy Women Daily
Instagram: @wealthywomendaily
Facebook: @wealthywomendaily
Facebook Investing Group: https://www.facebook.com/groups/wealthywomendaily

ABOUT CHARLENE RHINEHART

Charlene Rhinehart is a CPA, speaker, and published writer based in Chicago, IL. She is the founder of Wealthy Women Daily and the author of Dividends Are a Queen's Best Friend. She has served on the Financial Review Board for Investopedia and Chair of the Illinois CPA Society Individual Tax Committee. Charlene's financial insights have been published in national publications, including Black Enterprise, BlackDoctor.org, Essence Magazine, and AARP.

CHER'DON REYNOLDS

Written By: Kirby Wilson

Cher'Don Reynolds, believes life is about the impact that we make on the world. As SheEO of ShePrintsIt, LLC, Cher'Don makes a HUGE impact through her bulk apparel printing company which specializes in silk screens, heat transfers, and embroidery. It is her goal to provide the example she wanted to see when growing up. Along with running her highly sought-after company. Cher'Don is working on several projects devoted to mentoring women and teaching them industry staples such as promotional products and branding, as well as the power of self-love and determination.

Who is Cher'Don Reynolds?

I am a SheEO, mom and wife but most importantly She is Me. That simply means that I am focused on being my authentic self unapologetically with the hopes that I can empower the next generation of young girls to do the same. Life isn't about titles; it is about impact, and I strive to be a woman that leaves behind a legacy that will carry on for centuries.

Please tell us what being a business owner means to you and why you became an entrepreneur in the first place?

Being a business owner means that I can create jobs and opportunities for others. This is why I became an entrepreneur. I wanted to create a space where women felt safe, black people felt safe and all people felt financially sound. I never wanted to just be a high earner, I wanted to be a wealth creator for others.

What has been your greatest influence in business and why?

The person that has influenced me the most is my sister DeShawn Bullard. She has shown me that my dreams are possible. I have the privilege of having a front row seat in her journey as she built NouriTress from a one product brand in her basement to a 20 plus product line that has been featured in most major retail stores and internationally. She always tells me what I need to hear, not what I want to hear. I push to make her and my parents proud every day. I want to be the big sister to a world of women that she is to me.

What are three different strategies you would like to share with small business owners to increase their bottom line?

Always remember that success is in the Know, Like and Trust of your brand. Of course, you need strategy, plan and execution but if people don't know, like and trust you everything else means nothing. Know is not to just be present on social media but it's to show up in rooms where your target audience is. People need to see things 7 times before it's set to memory. Like is not about liking you but knowing what your audience likes. Take time to truly learn your avatar. And Trust is a big one. Transparency creates trust so tell your story, relate and be vulnerable sometimes, it's ok.

What does Women's History month mean to you?

Women's history month means that I have time to be seen and celebrated. Not for the titles that I hold to other people but for simply being me. I want young girls and grown women to know that they are enough. That they are amazing just as they are and if they want to change their hair, career, or any other thing about themselves that it's only to make themselves happy.

What upcoming projects do you have coming up?

I am working on several projects in my industry to teach and mentor other women that are interested in promotional products and product branding. We are also adding monthly crafting classes to our calendar of events at She Prints It. I'm also leaning into more speaking engagements with focus on the power of promotional products and "She is Me" the power of self-love.

Please tell readers how they can follow and support you on all social media platforms?

We are ShePrintsIt on all social media platforms and I have a personal Tik Tok account where I celebrate all things SHE and that SheisCher'Don.

ABOUT CHER'DON REYNOLDS
Cher'Don Reynolds is a dynamic entrepreneur, community leader, and trailblazer for women in business. A Chicago native who grew up in the Cabrini Green housing projects before moving to Atlanta to attend college, Cher'Don knows first-hand the struggles faced by those in underprivileged communities and understands the importance of overcoming adversity and persevering in the face of challenges. She has dedicated her life's work to empowering other women and helping them achieve success through their businesses, using the power of promotional products to increase revenue and build wealth.

As the SheEO of SHE PRINTS IT LLC, a fiercely female branding and promotional products company, Cher'Don is committed to supporting small businesses by helping them stay top-of-mind with their target market while maintaining their unique appeal. Her work has been recognized by several organizations and outlets, including the Community Leader award from Buy From a Black Woman foundation and the 2022 Access Taken Award from Classy Living Society, LLC. She Prints It has had the opportunity to provide promotional products for top corporate entities such IHG, Southern Company and Morehouse school of medicine to name a few. Her company has been featured in Sheen, PPAI Media, Voyage ATL, and many other publications. She has shared her story, business tips, and more as a speaker on the main stage of several conferences with the goal of inspiring women of all ages and backgrounds to believe in themselves and their brands. Additionally, in the wake of the COVID-19 pandemic, she established the My Sister's Keeper Grant to financially empower women-owned start-ups and small businesses.

Beyond her professional achievements, Cher'Don is also a devoted mother and wife who is deeply committed to creating a better world for her family and future generations. She truly lives by her creed that "There's room at the top for everyone, let's fill it up!" With her unwavering determination and entrepreneurial spirit, she is a shining example of the power of perseverance and the impact one person can have on their community

EVONYA EASLEY

Written By:
Kirby Wilson

Evonya Easley, Founder of Love E Fashion and Style by Love E, expands one of the greatest tools in your arsenal-style. She has over a decade of experience as a Certified Personal Stylist, Evonya creates looks that tell YOUR story as soon as you enter the room. With a great eye for fashion and a love for helping people create their best possible selves, Evonya sets the standard in the evolution of personally curated fashion for women of all ages, shapes, and sizes. A woman wearing an ensemble styled by Evonya brims with power and confidence. As she often says, "Clothes aren't going to change the world, the women who wear them will."

WOMEN ON THE MOVE

Who is Evonya Easley?

I am woman that loves supporting other women and empowering them to be their most confident selves at all times using personal style and image. I love to read, learn and travel the world, spend quality time with family and friends and amazing experiences. Im type A personality striving for excellence in all things and love and support my tribe to the fullest.

Please tell us what being a business owner means to you and why you became an entrepreneur in the first place?

I became an entrepreneur to turn my passion into profits full-time. I created my business to empower men and women to feel confident in how they show up in their personal and professional lives, and how that confidence has led them to accomplish their goals.

What has been your greatest influence in business and why?

Other successful women that have grown their businesses to multi millions and being able to make an impact on others, by seeing it is achievable makes it a possible reality for you.

What are three different strategies you would like to share with small business owners to increase their bottom line?

Building Relationships and networking is so important majority of my business has been from building authentic relationships with people that refer and advocate for me rooms I haven't been in yet.

Systems and Processes is so key to run your business efficiently and effectively. As a entrepreneur there is no boss or manager telling you what to do so you have to determine what to do to keep pushing the needle forward in your business so having systems and processes helps to know where you are head and progress being made.

Knowing your finances is so important to know where you been and where you are going to to set SMART goals, know when busy season or slow, what's selling what's not listening to your consumers and knowing their pain points to address them accordingly. Selling and marketing daily in some form or fashion thru different touch points like text, email, phone call, social media etc.

Why are you so passionate about fashion?

Fashion is a instant language it can express who you are and how you feel about yourself, as well as how others react to you, before you even open your mouth. Personal Style is a tool that can be used to help you achieve personal and professional goals. So I love being able to play a part in my clients lives and seeing their accomplishments come to life.

Where do you see Women in the fashion industry in the next five years?

I see women continuing to be leaders of major corporations and companies, lifting as we climb to bring more women on in positions of leadership, incorporating more tech and new ways for clients to have a better e-commerce and retail experience.

What does Women's History month mean to you?

Women's History to me is about celebrating the women that have paved the way and whose shoulders we stand on and the current women that are forging new paths with innovative ideas and executions.

What upcoming projects do you have coming up?

We are having an immersive one-of-a-kind fashion and shopping experience. Fusing fashion and technology, influential guests will be treated to their own personal 3D fashion show experience viewed through Meta's Oculus Quest 2 virtual reality headsets. The spring/summer collections of Black designers from across the country will be featured in the show as well as in the event space where attendees will have the opportunity to purchase the designs featured in the show while shopping other vendors and enjoying food, drink and live entertainment. https://loveefashion.com/generalandvip/

Please tell readers how they can follow and support you on all social media platforms?

Below is all my info to contact me :)

Evonya Easley, CEO/Founder
Love E Fashion/Styled by Love E
"Shine with Confidence & Style!"

Download our mobile app!
https://styledbylovee.com/
https://loveefashion.com/

Follow Us on Social Media!
https://www.instagram.com/styledbylovee/
https://www.instagram.com/loveevonya/

Work seen on MSNBC, CNN, Fox, Bloomberg, Disney, VH-1 & more!

ABOUT EVONYA EASLEY

"Love E" Evonya Easley is a certified personal stylist and published author has over a decade of experience in personal styling and the fashion industry. She has worked with hundreds of clients to achieve their personal best including NY Fashion Week, TBS, Fox, HLN, CNN, MSNBC, Vh-1, and Disney just to name a few. She is also the founder and CEO of Styled by Love E, a personal styling on demand mobile app for busy professional men and women, where a personal stylist can be ordered to shop, deliver and style you; giving our clients the armor of confidence that a good wardrobe can provide. Our expert stylists bring unique pieces that can be paired with your staples, saving our clients time and making shopping convenient. Look good and feel confident at every size, stage and transition in your life. Evonya believes in empowering men and women through their wardrobe enabling them to show up as their most confident selves in their professional and personal lives.

ASHLEYLITTLEENTERPRISES.COM

SYLVIA HIGH

Written By:
Gracia Collins Rich

Impact Speaker and Founder/CEO of Aiming High, Inc, Sylvia High wants us to stop playing small and live the BIG life we are created for. Sylvia is a Master Coach, Training and Development Strategist and Author with over three decades of success. She assists individuals to thrive in a competitive business atmosphere and their personal lives. Her latest book, I Am Woman: Devotional for Elevated Living, designed to guide individuals in a rich self-reflection by using pointed questions and provocative insights, in order for participants to take actions that will bring about their desired results. Sylvia believes "We are always just one conversation away from transformation," and with her I AM WOMAN Conference these conversations happen transforming the lives of women throughout the country; elevating the WHOLE woman, big heart, mind, and spirit.

WOMEN ON THE MOVE

Who is Sylvia High?

Sylvia High, founder of Aiming High Inc., is a Transformational Trainer, and Development Strategist with over 30 years of success.

Sylvia coached thousands of people and hundreds of organizations to achieve unprecedented results. Throughout her experience, Sylvia partnered with amazing organizations such as Uber, Squarespace, Delta, Brown-Forman, and LinkedIn.

Also known by many as 'The Gap Closer', Sylvia gets people from where they are, to where they want to be by identifying the blind spots that block their unique success.

Sylvia's astounding ability to coach the 'nuances' that limit a person's success placed her on world platforms such as Bishop TD Jakes, at MEGAFest, Comcast's Coaches Camp, and Oprah's Live Your Life Tour.

Sylvia authored The Little Book of Big Questions: A Journey in Self Discovery and I Am Woman: Devotional for Elevated Living, designed to guide individuals in a rich self-reflection by using pointed questions and provocative insights, in order for participants to take actions that will bring about their desired results.

Sylvia serves as curator of the amazing annual I Am Woman Conference; a multicultural two-day experience designed to empower and ignite women.

She is a big hearted, big minded, big spirited woman who resides in the San Francisco Bay Area.

Please tell us what being a business owner means to you and why you became an entrepreneur in the first place?

Being a Black and Woman-owned business gave me the freedom to use my God-given gifts in order to impact and help make the world a better place. Being an entrepreneur is one of the most impactful ways I can empower humanity to live their best life.

What has been your greatest influence in business and why?

Watching others' belief in self-growth and the privilege of supporting them achieving their dreams and goals. It fuels me in my work to make a positive difference in the spaces I occupy and world.

What are three different strategies you would like to share with small business owners to increase their bottom line?

1) Know your WHY.

ASHLEYLITTLEENTERPRISES.COM

WOMEN ON THE MOVE

2) Know WHY YOU.

3) Have an infrastructure that supports success.

Why are you so passionate about helping businesses and women thrive in competitive environments?

As an entrepreneur for over 30 years, I have seen the ups and downs, ins and out of talented people struggle without the confidence and know-how. Every time a woman is empowered and wields her ability to take a dream into reality, the world benefits. Their families, workplaces, communities benefit.

I was taught what is given, must is expected. I believe in Ghandi's expression that we must be the change we wish to see, instead of asking why or look to someone else. I know that "I'm that someone" and we should always positively impact the spaces we occupy.

Please tell readers more about the I AM WOMAN Conference, and how they can support and attend?

IAW 2023 BELIEVE: www.iamwomanconference.com

This year is the ninth annual event - a two-day, multicultural experience designed to empower leading women and emerging leaders. It is designed to be a high-impact breakthrough weekend that's interactive, life-changing, game changing to shift how women see and experience themselves. I Am Woman is a curated experienced for the whole woman - big heart, mind, and spirit.

Women leave with tools and get in action with their dreams and visions AT the conference and CONTINUE those actions after the conference. Each year, women come back with energized with testimonials, progress, & results from achieving goals that were only dreamt of in their lives prior to attending. I Am Woman edifies the soul, it is a spirit lifter, while annihilating and breaking historical limiting beliefs.

What does Women's History month mean to you?

It's a beautiful opportunity to highly and celebrate the power, contribution, and abilities. We get to and deserve to be heard everything and Women's History month is icing on the cake that acknowledges our voice being heard.

What upcoming projects do you have coming up?

On February 1, I am a Panelist for the In Pursuit of Dreams Series in association with the Advancement of Blacks in Sports. This amazing panel composed of me, with Keshia Knight-Pulliam and others will focus on The Path to Greatness Lies Within.

On February 8, I am launching JOURNEY TO EXTRAORDINARY, the ninth installment of a four-week, virtual coaching journey designed to put individuals in the seat of their power and create unprecedented, personal success.

On February 9-12, I am a Panelist for Train the Trainer with Momentum Education, a four-day retreat for participants to gain the tools and confidence to build their brand and powerfully share their story.

On March 25-26, is my signature coaching experience, Supercharge. It is a two-day, 12-person mastermind designed for high achievers to identify and operate in alignment with their unique Genius.

Please tell readers how they can follow and support you on all social media platforms?

Instagram, Facebook, and LinkedIn: @SylviaHigh
Tiktok: aiminghighwithsylviahigh
Website: www.aiminghighinc.com

ABOUT SYLVIA HIGH

Sylvia High, founder of Aiming High Inc., two-time Author, Master Coach, Transformational Trainer, and a Development Strategist with nearly 30 years of success, delivering content and context to help businesses and individuals thrive in any competitive environment.

Sylvia was featured in ESSENCE Magazine, Huffington Post and Black Enterprise. As an Impact Speaker, Sylvia was a panelist of the Oprah's Live Your Life Tour, including Bishop TD Jakes, MEGAFest, BET Network's Leading Women Defined Conference and keynote for CISCO's Women of Impact Conference.

AUTHOR ON THE RISE

AIRNECIA MILLS

Written By: Gracia Rich Collins

Best Selling Author Airnecia Mills, has always had a passion for children and education. As an educator and Founder of Mills Academy, a comprehensive academic tutoring center in Greenville, Mississippi. Airnecia shares her love by offering unique opportunities for students in her area. In 2020, the Pandemic made virtual education a must. Mills Academy Book Vending Machine, became the ultimate reading resource for students of all ages. Airnecia uses her triumph over Endometriosis to encourage other women who may be battling the same obstacle in her new book Beyond the Smile. An avid writer, Airnecia was thrilled to be able to express herself through the written word and connect with women who have similar experiences. She looks forward to connecting with more women in the near future through conferences regarding Endometriosis.

Who is Airnecia Mills?

Airnecia Mills is a native of Greenville, Mississippi. She attended Alcorn State University where she was actively involved in Student Government. During her undergraduate studies, she was a member of the Alcorn State Cheer Team, served as a Student Ambassador, became a member of Alpha Kappa Alpha Sorority, Inc., and was crowned Miss Alcorn State University, 2012-2013. She earned a Bachelor of Science degree in Elementary Education in 2013, and a Master of Science degree in Education with Reading and Special Education endorsements in 2015, both from Alcorn State University. She continued her advanced studies at Arkansas State University where she graduated in 2020, with a Specialist Degree in Educational Leadership. Airnecia currently is pursuing a doctoral degree in Educational Leadership at Belhaven University, Jackson, Mississippi. Presently, she serves as the Assistant Principal at Lockard Elementary School in Sunflower County, Mississippi.

Airnecia is the owner and founder of Mills Academy, a comprehensive after school tutoring and academic learning center in Greenville, MS. In 2020, virtual learning provided an opportunity for Airnecia to expand her quest to educate students. She expanded her portfolio by acquiring Mills Academy Book Vending Machine as an immediate resource to provide a wide breadth of reading resources for students of all grades and ages. In 2022, Airnecia was recognized as Woman of the Year for the Enterprise Toscan. She continued to pursue dreams and achieve goals with the release of her biography, "Beyond the Smile."

In her spare time, Airnecia finds immense pleasure in reading and researching, tutoring, helping others, and mentoring young girls. She basks in frequent travels and explores parts of the Unites States and other countries. When asked about her journey, Airnecia readily acknowledges that she is grateful for the many blessings to personally grow as she impacts and influences the lives of others.

Airnecia, you are the Author of the new book!! Beyond The Smile. Please tell readers more about your book.

It has always been my desire to write about something that can motivate and encourage others. People will never know the battles I deal with silently when they see me because I am always smiling. My smile is not to hide my pain; it is to choose happiness in spite of it. My book, "Beyond the Smile" shares my struggles with Endometriosis and how I overcame them. I enlighten women on endometriosis and encourage them to push through. Endometriosis is an often-painful disorder in which the tissue that lines the inside of your uterus, the endometrium, grows outside your uterus. Writing the book was so much fun. I felt that I was able to express myself and tell my story.

Please tell readers more about your passion for writing.

I believe that writing helps me to express myself. Writing also helps me to reflect on past experiences and put my thoughts into words. I fell deeper in love with writing in 2021 when I became a contributing author to "The HBCU Experience: The HBCU Royal Queens 2nd Edition". I was so grateful to have a chapter in the book and to be a contributing author, sharing my experience as an HBCU Queen. This experience encouraged me to write my own book.

Airnecia, what do you want readers to take away from your new book?

I want readers to know that they can still live a great life even if they suffer from Endometriosis or other health issues. There are ways to cope with the issue and continue to strive for greatness. Giving up is not an option. Instead, persist despite the magnitude of your pain or struggle. The battle of your life is not meant to bring you down. It is not meant to defeat you. It is meant to build your character and to help you become a fighter-resilient, persistent, and knowledgeable. There is purpose in your journey. God will use your pain and turn it into a life vest to help other women cope with their issues. Your testimony may be the light and hope that someone may need to feel less alone in his or her struggle.

Please tell readers what upcoming projects you have coming up?

I have so many plans for myself. I dream big and work hard, but I pray about my dreams and goals and let God lead the way. This year, 2023, I will graduate from Belhaven University with my doctorate in Educational Leadership and relocate from Mississippi to Washington, DC. My goal is to continue to climb the ladder in education, moving up from Assistant Principal to Principal while impacting children and adults and helping them to grow. I will continue to give back to my hometown because Greenville, also known as "The Heart of the Delta", made me who I am today. I will continue my journey as an author and write more inspirational and motivational books. It's very therapeutic and rewarding. Using my book, Beyond the Smile, I plan to travel to conferences and workshops to share my story with many women who are struggling with Endometriosis.

How can our readers follow and support you?

Readers can follow and support in the following ways:

Personal Website: www.airneciamills.com
Facebook: Airnecia Mills
Instagram: airnecia_mills
Linked In: Airnecia Mills
Email Address: Airnecia@yahoo.com

future millennial MILLIONAIRE

CHEYLAINA FULTZ

Written By: Gracia Collins Rich

HBCU Legacy Fashion Founder/CEO Cheylaina Fultz is daring us to BE our true selves. Her entrepreneurial journey began in 2012 as a wedding and event planner, Cheylaina has always believed in capturing the moments that make life incredible. Through her sensational media platform, The Cheylaina Fultz Talk Show, she brings wisdom, encouragement, and grit of women entrepreneurs who have navigated obstacles to become powerhouse leaders. Cheylaina is a formidable force for the future.

ASHLEYLITTLEENTERPRISES.COM

FUTURE MILLENNIAL MILLIONAIRE

Who is Cheylaina Fultz?

I am tenacious, an overcomer, a go-getter with a plan to prove the naysayers wrong while creating an empire and legacy for my children's children. In addition to being the Founder & CEO of HBCU Legacy Fashion, I am the host of The Cheylaina Fultz Talk Show where I share stories of women who have overcome challenges just as I have and evolved into amazing entrepreneurs and powerful leaders. I challenge women to punch imposter syndrome in the face so they can confidently walk into their purpose and be all that God has called them to be.

Please tell us what being a business owner means to you and why you became an entrepreneur in the first place?

Being a business owner means being able to leave your footprint on the earth in an extremely impactful way. It means creating not only generational, but sustainable wealth for your family and loved ones as well as being a resource to do the same for the people who work for you. I grew up amongst entrepreneurs and business owners, so there was never a doubt in my mind that I would become one too. I never dreamed of working for a Fortune 500 company, instead I dreamed of building one.

Please tell readers about your business what product or service you provide and who your target audience is?

HBCU Legacy Fashion helps those with HBCU pride display the spirit of their school through high quality fashion by increasing the opportunity to make a fashion statement, and reducing the time spent customizing their children's outfits. We design matching apparel for you and your little HBCU legacy that won't easily fade, but instead it can be passed down through generations like an heirloom. The HBCU Legacy Fashion collection includes embroidered denim jackets, sequin bomber jackets and beautifully embroidered sweatshirts, onesies, rompers and more. When you support HBCU Legacy Fashion, you invest in the next generation of HBCU graduates as 12% of your purchase goes back to the institution.

Where do you see HBCU Legacy in the next five years?

Within the next five years, HBCU Legacy Fashion will be in all of your favorite retail and department stores, creating partnerships with big brands as we continue our mission to bring awareness to HBCUs by increasing their endowment funds through our royalty sales. We will also host annual galas to raise money for The HBCU Legacy Scholarship fund which is our nonprofit 501(c)(3).

What are three wealth building strategies you would like to share with millennials who are aspiring to take their businesses to the next level and increase their bottom line?

Because I am a "*creative*" at my core, someone who has a million ideas a day, it's been hard for me to not do "*all of the things*." However, through coaching, and my own burn out, I've learned that it's imperative to focus on one thing at a time. And while it's okay to be multipassionate (as I am), you are only one person and cannot be successful if you're trying to grow multiple businesses at once but haven't even mastered the first one. Keep the main thing the main thing. You will burn out and sabotage the momentum you've built for those many projects if you try to do them all at one time. This is why in 2020 I made the decision to pivot out of my service-based wedding planning business to my product based HBCU Legacy Fashion business. Focus on one business or project at a time and grow it.

Take a pizza shop for example: Is Dominos, Pizza Hut, Papa Johns, Unos, or any other pizza joint known for wings, mozzarella sticks, a salad, or a sub? Of course not. But do they offer it? Yes, they do! And if they're known for pizza, why do they offer those extra items on their menu? Because they mastered their secret sauce (pun intended)! They got good at making pizza that their target audience craved. Then, they were able to scale and add on other money makers (i.e. The salads, subs, wings, and desserts). Get your business to the point where you have mastered YOUR secret sauce and can now afford to have a team help you scale. You've heard that you should have 7 streams of income. While I strive to get there, I know those streams have to be a gradual add on. I'm sure you've also heard the phrase, "jack of all trades, master of none." So, my

ASHLEYLITTLEENTERPRISES.COM

first suggestion is to get good at formulating your secret sauce, master your trade, then grow! Secondly, if you're a product-based e-commerce business, I'd suggest wholesaling. You want to be able to offer your product to multiple retailers. Have a line sheet of all of your products ready with images, wholesale and suggested retail costs should be listed. Pitch these to retailers who align with your values and have your target market. (That's another thing, make sure you always have a great pitch ready.) The real money with a product-based business is going to come in the form of wholesaling. Don't know where to start with finding the contacts? Join quality communities for business owners. Get on LinkedIn. It's a free treasure! You'll be amazed with how many genuine connections you can make as a business owner. Long gone are the days of LinkedIn only being a place to find a job. It's a tool to grow and scale your business if you use it right. (Tip: Make sure you've created a LinkedIn page for your business, too.)

Thirdly, make sure you are building your business on a strong foundation. Have a business plan, marketing plan, mission statement, customer segments (no more than 3 to start with), value proposition and your SOPs (standard operating procedures) written out. Having established systems and processes are so very important if you plan to grow a team. Your team will need to be able to reference some type of material to properly get their work done and to effectively save you time… after all, that is why you hired them. But if they have to constantly ask you how to do something, you will both become frustrated. I suggest the next time you're working on anything that you plan to give to a new hire, document the steps. You can do this with screenshots and written direction for each step, screen recordings, or you may also set up your tripod with a ring light and record yourself completing a task and narrating the instructions for each step.

Please tell readers about your upcoming projects and how they can support?

We'll be on the road again vending (especially in the fall for homecoming season). Follow me on IG to keep up with upcoming projects. You can also subscribe to The Cheylaina Fultz Talk Show anywhere you listen to your podcasts and please subscribe to my YouTube channel [YouTube.com/TheCheylainaFultzTalkShow].

Please tell readers how they can follow and support you on all social media platforms?

I mostly hangout on Instagram @CheylainaFultz and Linkedin at linkedin.com/in/cheylainafultz. You can support HBCU Legacy Fashion by following us on Instagram.com/HBCULegacyFashion and by letting all of your HBCU friends and supporters know we exist to extend the legacy of their HBCU through our licensed HBCU apparel for mommy and me plus daddy and me!

ABOUT CHEYLAINA FULTZ

Cheylaina Fultz may have been raised as a small town girl, but she has always had big city dreams with an entrepreneurial spirit, and a passion for acting and media.

She is a proud 2008 graduate of North Carolina A&T State University where she pledged Alpha Kappa Alpha Sorority, Incorporated, and obtained a degree in Journalism & Mass Communication with a concentration in Journalism & Electronic Media.

For over 10 years, Cheylaina planned weddings and events nationally and internationally. This led her to create The Cheylaina Fultz Talk Show, a podcast that shares stories of women who have overcome opposition and evolved into amazing entrepreneurs and powerful leaders.

In 2020, Cheylaina pivoted into the fashion industry and launched HBCU Legacy Fashion, where her licensed HBCU apparel fashionably connects youth to the historic legacy of HBCUs while also yielding royalties to partner institutions. The whole family can display the spirit of their school with the mommy and me plus daddy and me lines.

In 2022, HBCU Legacy Fashion was selected into the inaugural cohort of Goldman Sach's 1 Million Black Women in Business: Black in Business program. HBCU Legacy Fashion is currently working on its next big move, wholesaling to department stores with a fall 2023 launch into retail.

Today, Cheylaina is a wife, mom of three, CEO, author, and talkshow host residing in Columbus, Ohio. She enjoys meeting and interviewing new people, acting, emceeing events, and traveling to a beach with a good book in hand.

HEALTH & WELLNESS, FAITH & INSPIRATION, & MENTAL HEALTH CORNERS

MENTAL HEALTH corner

UNDERSTANDING THE DIFFERENCE BETWEEN SADNESS AND SIGNS OF DEPRESSION.

Written By Dr. Kerry-Ann Zamore

There are varying experiences, which can be difficult for a person to endure. The death of a loved one, loss of a job or the ending of a relationship are all experiences which contributes to normal feelings of sadness or grief. Those experiencing loss often might describe themselves as being "depressed." But being sad is not the same as a diagnosis of depression. The grieving process is natural, unique to each individual and has some of the same features of depression. Grief and depression may involve intense feelings of sadness and withdrawal or lack of motivation for usual activities. They are also different in important ways:
In grief, painful feelings come in waves, often intermixed with positive memories of the deceased. In depression, mood and/or interest (pleasure) are decreased for most of two weeks. In grief, self-esteem is usually maintained. In depression, feelings of worthlessness and self-loathing are common.

In grief, thoughts of death may surface when thinking of or fantasizing about "joining" the deceased loved one. In depression, thoughts are focused on ending one's life due to feeling worthless or undeserving of living or being unable to cope with the pain of depression.
Understanding the differences between grief and depression is important in identifying if additional or professional support is needed. If sadness is prolonged, invasive thoughts become more frequent, or a person withdraws from participating in activities generally enjoyed; then do follow up with a mental health provider.

When in doubt – CALL 988 (Suicide support line) or your local, state or national assistance line for support.

FAITH & INSPIRATION corner

ENDURE

Written By: Dr. Nancy Joy Dozier

"The race Is not given to the swift but to the one who endures until the end." Although this saying has widely become accepted as a proverb, it is a Biblical truth that is worth examining, especially as a new year begins. No doubt that quotas, productivity reports, projections, trends and goals have already arrested most of our focus thus far in 2023. Many are already in "beast mode", pushing themselves to compete and surpass their counterparts, or even their own previous personal successes. There is nothing wrong with pushing for more. Growth is essential, but the journey to growth can have either positive or negative impact. Breaking out and pushing through at the start of the year can initiate a pace that is not sustainable. This can lead to stress and anxiety, which in turn impedes the ability to finish strong. But If we accurately discern our output and correctly manage our energy, we will endure to the end. This can be the year that you don't burn out by July, if you embrace wisdom and settle Into a healthy pace now. This can be a year where you gain healthy momentum and enjoy the journey of growth all year long, if you don't allow yourself to be pressured by the need to perform. Embrace a rhythm that you can sustain. Remember to breathe, you've got this.

HEALTH & WELLNESS corner

HOW BUSINESS OWNERS CAN STAY HEALTHY DURING A RECESSION

Written By: Brittany Ramsey, Fitness Expert, Speaker, and Mindset Coach

As a Fitness Professional, with over a decade of experience, I have seen a huge decline in the health of business owners during this recession. Recessions can have a significant impact on the mental and physical health of business owners. The stress of financial uncertainty and potential loss of income can lead to anxiety and depression. Additionally, the long hours and lack of work-life balance that often come with running a business can worsen existing health issues.

Therefore I want to share with you how business owners like yourself, can stay healthy during a recession. First, it is important to prioritize self-care and maintain a healthy work-life balance. This can include making time for exercise and physical activity, eating a balanced diet, getting enough sleep, and engaging in activities that bring you joy and relaxation.

Another important tip to stay healthy during a recession is to maintain a positive mindset and focus on solutions rather than dwelling on problems. This can involve setting clear goals and making a plan to achieve them. It's also important to take care of your mental health during this time, you can try different techniques such as meditation, yoga, or mindfulness; it can help you to keep calm and avoid excessive stress.

If you are a career woman, entrepreneur, or leader who wants to take back your health, so you can stay on a consistent fitness and nutrition schedule, I created a specialized technique to get you massive results in 2 months of working with me.

The same techniques that I use to develop award winning bodies, I will teach you too, so you can achieve results in this short time! If you're determined with major body goals and you're ready to get started with a plan, without all the guesswork, so you can tone up and lose 10-20lbs or more in the next 8 weeks, click here for a complimentary health assessment with me.

https://square.site/book/25APTTEJ420NX/msfitbritt-llc-bolingbrook-il

FASHION, KIDPRENEUR CORNERS

FASHION Corner

SHOW UP IN STYLE
Written By: Elle Renée

Whether you started your entrepreneurial journey one day ago or five years ago, you would agree that the list of things to do continuously grows. The opportunity to keep your lists and thoughts free of "what to wear" is easier than you think. Where you show up and when you show up may change, but exercising freedom to infuse your personal style in how you show up remains the same.

Here are two ways an entrepreneur can show up in style:

1) Suited for success.

Even with ever evolving fashion rules, the opportunity to only make one great first impression is one rule that has not changed. The return on investment (ROI) for owning a suit that can be worn in any season is high. Whether you choose a pantsuit or a skirt suit, selecting a neutral color is wise too. When the occasion welcomes fashion freedom, transform your look by adding accessories and pops of color using scarves, broaches, tops or belts.

2) Sole Statement.

Shoes can tell a lot about a person's style. The days of wearing dull and boring shoes are over. From heels, pumps, flats, clogs, loafers, wedges, to boots and booties, they all come in great colors, heights and patterns. Do not be afraid to wear prints or patterns on your soles. Just like a classic suit, invest in a quality pair of neutral colored shoes. With every move you make and every step you take, do it in style.

Now that you have a few tips on how to show up in style on your entrepreneurial journey, start building a wardrobe with pieces that not only reflect your current style, but where you aspire to be. Remember, dress how you want to be addressed.

ABOUT THE AUTHOR
Elle Renée is a personal stylist and image consultant. Founder of Hoosier Stylist & Image Consultant, Elle Renée helps entrepreneurs, experts and executives create wardrobes that reflect their ambition, brilliance and confidence in style. Connect with Elle Renée @hoosierstylist on FB and IG or www.HoosierStylist.com

YOUR PERSONAL STYLE
Written By: Danielle Marshall "The Style Marshall"

What do your clothes say about you? What purpose do you serve in your field of work? What position do you hold? How do you present yourself in excellence?

"Style is knowing what suits you, who you are, and what your assets are. It's accepting it all." – Bianca Jagger

Your expression of style and choice of attire says a lot about you before you even speak. When you prepare for your day, are you choosing your outfit based on your mood, the company requirement, or your personal style? Our moods are constantly changing so this may not be the best approach. With your calendar in front of you, try preparing your outfits before a new week begins. This way, you are not rushing the day of, trying to figure out what to wear and if it needs maintenance.

If your office has a certain dress code, you should adhere to the guidelines but creatively add some flair and edge. Explore new colors and mild prints that work with your body type and won't bring too much attention to you.

Just keep in mind to be intentional with your personal style. Authenticity is key.

There is only one you so make each outfit count! Danielle "The Style Marshall"

KIDPRENEUR Corner

Celebrate!

It's time to celebrate all of what you have done and what will become. Each step in the process of achieving your goals is a reason to celebrate. Whether big or small achievements, it's an accomplishment and should be celebrated. No one can tell you what path or what decisions to make when it's your vision. All of your hard work will pay off in the beginning… celebrate, in the middle… celebrate and at the end… celebrate. Celebration matters and you matter!! Celebrate YOU all of 2023!!! Keep going and reaching for the stars… and Celebrate!

-Bailey Reese Moore

KIDPRENUER

Aminah Rose

Written By: Gracia Collins Rich

Multi-talented Aminah Rose is more than a Kidpreneur, she is a BOSS! Founder of Aminah Rose, LLC and POSE by Aminah Rose, this seven year old phenom is taking the fashion industry by storm, one stunning ensemble at a time. Through her fashion line, POSE by Aminah Rose, she creates beautifully curated styles for kids that inspire confidence from head to toe. One successful show under her belt, this aspiring fashion designer and runway model is gearing up for her summer show as we speak. Aminah is clearly shooting for the stars and shining brilliantly.

Who is Aminah Rose?

I am the seven-year-old mini fashion mogul and Founder of Aminah Rose, LLC and POSE by Aminah Rose. I am an aspiring fashion designer and runway model. I am a straight A student from Florence, South Carolina. I am amazing. I am fierce. I am pretty. I am smart, and I am not afraid to chase my dreams.

Please tell us what being a Kidpreneur means to you and why you became a kidpreneur in the first place?

Having my own business is important to me because I get to do what I love and it's kind of like having my own job, even as a kid, but I get to be my own boss! I decided to start my own business because I want to be a fashion designer when I grow up and I want to share my fashionable, beautiful styles with people all around the world.

Why are you so passionate about fashion and modeling?

I love fashion because It's pretty and I love unique styles and designs. I love modeling because I love to show people my fashionable clothes and I love to POSE!

Please tell readers more about POSE by Aminah Rose?

POSE by Aminah Rose is the name of my first fashion line as well as my new fashion show and it's all about making other kids like me feel so happy and confident! I came up with the name POSE because I have been posing since I was two years old, and I want to inspire other people to POSE too!

Congratulations!! on your inaugural fashion show please tell readers more about it and how they can support?

ASHLEYLITTLEENTERPRISES.COM

KIDPRENUER | AMINAH ROSE

Thank you! My last fashion show was a lot of fun. I had other kid vendors, a dance team, a DJ, and over 20 kid models who modeled in three different categories. My favorite part was the models because they looked so cute in their clothes! My Summer Fashion Show is next, and I am already casting models, girls and boys, ages 3-12! Readers can support by visiting my website to register kid models for the Summer Show and subscribing to my website for updates on ticket release.

Please tell readers how they follow and support you on all social media platforms?

You can follow my modeling pages on Facebook and Instagram: @poseaminahrose

You can follow the boutique on Facebook and Instagram: @shopaminahrose

You can keep up with my brand and all of my new ventures on my website: www.aminahrose.com

For bookings or other inquiries, you can email info@aminahrose.com

ABOUT AMINAH ROSE
Aminah is a seven-year-old model and inspiration behind the brand, POSE by Aminah Rose. Aminah decided to name her brand POSE because of her deep passion for dressing to impress, modeling and posing for every camera. With an early eye for fashion since the age of two, the young mogul has expressed her love and desire to enhance every look and rock it with confidence and flair. As a young toddler, Aminah took to fashion in a unique way. She refused to go out of the house, even just to daycare, unless she had on an outfit that made her feel her absolute best! She loves to take photos and serve as many poses as she can in every look!

Aminah later channeled her love for fashion into her own special business ventures, starting with making paper purses in a variety of designs, patterns, and accessories and selling them to her supporters! Her first venture taught her many of the ins and outs of doing business, to include keeping up with inventory as well as the cost of shipping and supplies! Her love for fashion and having her own business continued to grow with time! She asked for her own sewing machine for Christmas at just the age of five and began to take sewing lessons with her grandmother. She started by purchasing a variety of prints and sewing her own clothes. She then learned how to make mini pillows, which she began to sell and ship to her supporters in various styles and colors! After years of developing a personal brand and modeling experience, she launched Aminah Rose, LLC (www.aminahrose.com), a luxury children's boutique, to share her passion with young girls around the world.

Aminah believes that girls run the world, and their superpowers are instantly unlocked when they look and feel their best each day. Aminah's first fashion line, "POSE," offers luxury apparel in girls sizes 4-10. Through her boutique, she strongly believes she can unleash self-confidence in young girls around the world! Aminah quickly began to pursue her next venture. The mini mogul is the curator of the semi-annual POSE by Aminah Rose Fashion Show in Florence, SC. This high-demand, groundbreaking experience displays the latest fashion trends and seasonal collections, showcased by youth models ages 3-12. Girls and boys display wearable art and share fashion inspiration with confidence and poise down a 60 ft. runway!

Aminah's first fashion show was a sold out event and she has already begun planning her Summer 2023 show, which is now casting models and designers! Aminah Rose is also set to launch her Spring fashion line in April 2023 and also has some exciting new business ventures that are soon to come! She plans to continue expanding her brand while opening doors for children in her area who dream big and love fashion & design, just like her! Aminah's goal is to become a fashion designer & mogul in the fashion industry at a

www.ingramcontent.com/pod-product-compliance
Lightning Source LLC
Chambersburg PA
CBHW051952210526
45473CB00023B/933